Psychiatric Topics for Community Workers

SIGNS OF STRESS
the social problems of psychiatric illness

PSYCHIATRIC TOPICS for community workers
General Editor: Alistair Munro
Psychiatrist-in-Chief, University of Toronto

Left Behind: a study of mental handicap
Dr. *W. Alan Heaton-Ward*, Stoke Park Group of Hospitals, Bristol

Insanity: a study of major psychiatric disorders
Professor R. G. Priest, St. Mary's Hospital Medical School, London
Dr. J. Steinert, Springfield Hospital, London

Alcoholism and Addiction
Dr. R. Swinson, Toronto General Hospital
Dr. Derek Eaves, Western Regional Medical Centre, British Columbia

Growing Pains: a study of teenage distress
Dr. Edna M. Irwin, Hollymoor Hospital, Birmingham

Signs of Stress: the social problems of psychiatric illness
J. Wallace McCulloch, University of Bradford
Herschel A. Prins, University of Leicester

SIGNS OF STRESS
the social problems of psychiatric illness

J. Wallace McCulloch
Senior Lecturer
School of Applied Social Studies,
University of Bradford

Herschel A. Prins
Senior Lecturer
School of Social Work,
University of Leicester

THE WOBURN PRESS

This edition published 1978 in Great Britain by
THE WOBURN PRESS
Gainsborough House, Gainsborough Road,
London E11 1RS, England

and in the United States of America by
THE WOBURN PRESS
c/o Biblio Distribution Centre
81 Adams Drive, P.O. Box 327, Totowa, N.J. 07511

Copyright © 1978 J. Wallace McCulloch and Herschel A. Prins

ISBN 0 7130 0165 8

All rights reserved. No part of this publication may be reproduced in any form or by any means, electronic, mechanical, photocopying, recording or otherwise, without the prior permission of The Woburn Press in writing.

Text set in 11/12 pt Photon Times, printed by photolithography, and bound in Great Britain at The Pitman Press, Bath

We wish to acknowledge much encouragement and kindly advice from the editor of this series—Professor Alistair Munro; also from Mr. D. A. F. Sutherland of the publishers. We owe a special debt of gratitude to Miss Sarah Prins, not only for typing our manuscript with such care, but for the correction whilst doing so, of some of our more gross grammatical errors. Finally our thanks to our wives and families who tolerated our absences from domestic responsibilities so uncomplainingly. To them, this book is dedicated with affection and thanks.

J. W. M.
H. A. P.

Contents

1 Possession – containment – tolerance? 17
2 Mental health and mental illness 34
3 The neuroses 45
4 The functional psychoses 68
5 Psychiatric conditions due to old age or organic disorders 87
6 Abnormalities of personality and psychosexual disorders 104
7 The problems of drugs and alcohol 123
8 Social aspects of suicidal behaviour 140
9 Mental subnormality (mental handicap) 158
10 The legal aspects of psychiatric disorders 175
11 General discussion and conclusions 191
   Index

Editor's Foreword

One of the questions constantly being asked of a psychiatrist is, 'Are mental illnesses on the increase?' A second is, 'Do you think the stress of modern living is responsible for the increase in mental illness?'

To take the second question first: no one will persuade me that, for the average individual in a Western country, modern living is more stressful than it was for his parents or his grandparents. We all have our private difficulties and sorrows, but at the present time, the average man's expectations for long life and good health are greater than ever before. In fact, we are now at a stage where certain illnesses are the result of affluence rather than deprivation: for example, overeating leads to obesity, hypertension and heart-disease; excessive smoking to lung cancer; and excessive drinking to alcoholism. We may persuade ourselves that we have fundamental worries, but many of today's problems come nowhere near the life-and-death level of those experienced by previous generations. So, I take more than a little convincing that mental illness is due to the increased pace of modern life.

Returning to the first question: are mental illnesses really on the increase? Drug-dependence is increasing, and so is affluence alcoholism. Psychiatric disorders of old age are rapidly increasing in numbers, but this is largely because so many more people are surviving into extreme old age. But so far as the great bulk of psychiatric illness is concerned, there is no very good evidence that it is substantially on the increase and there are actually some conditions – particularly those due to organic brain-disease in younger individuals – which have dramatically decreased as medical science has learned to combat the underlying disorder.

Then why, if they are not increasing markedly, does there

seem to be so much more concern and publicity about psychiatric illness nowadays? The answer to this is a complex one, but one very important reason lies in the great success that medicine has had in preventing or curing so many serious, crippling or even fatal physical illnesses. In a society where life is mean, disease rife and death common – and this is a fair description of life for a considerable bulk of our population until comparatively recent times – most people have little opportunity to stop and question the quality of their existence and illness has to be patently serious before it is paid much notice.

Psychiatric illness has probably always been common but until relatively recently, it was only the most florid varieties, which resulted in 'insanity', which were recognised as such. All the rest either had to be suffered or else the sufferer had to risk being called 'morally weak', 'a malingerer', or worse. Nowadays we have the opportunity, and increasingly the skill, to see these conditions for what they are and realisation has grown of the enormous amount of anguish they cause, both to the individual patient and to the community as a whole. They can be seen as illnesses, not mysterious, but with demonstrable causes, characteristic patterns of development and, more and more, responsiveness to treatment.

It is impossible to deny the reality of psychiatric illness, though some misguided people still try. Its commonness is staggering, though fortunately the great mass of it is of fairly minor degrees of severity. Nowadays, psychiatric complaints are among the most frequent made to general practitioners, and a growing proportion of the resources of the Health and Social Services is being devoted to dealing with them. Psychiatry is now one of the largest medical specialties and the demands made upon its practitioners are ever-increasing. It is a straightforward and workaday branch of medicine with a growing ability to recognise mental illness at an early stage and to intervene successfully with treatment.

Despite its greater effectiveness, psychiatry is still looked at askance by many people, and mental illness still bears a stigma and an aura of superstitious fear long ago lost by most physical diseases. It is high time that these medieval attitudes disappeared for ever and accurate knowledge is one way to disperse them. Another way to defeat them is to show unequivocally that psychiatric illness is treatable: cholera and typhus used to strike terror into people's hearts but now we look on them simply as physical diseases to be tackled with rational treatment, and we should be adopting the same attitude towards mental disorder.

Let me repeat: psychiatry is a branch of medicine. It is not mumbo-jumbo, its methods are neither mysterious nor magical. But if people think they are, then it is time they were informed otherwise. Most of us are fascinated with matters of the mind and many people find illnesses of the mind a compelling, if at times disturbing, subject. This book, which is one of a series on psychiatric illness, takes a cool but compassionate look at the whole field of psychiatric disorder and, in the process, I think it rips away some of the veils of obscurity surrounding it.

The series is not primarily designed for medical men, though we hope some of them may read it with interest and profit. Rather, it is designed for the concerned layman – a very wide term. It has been authoritatively calculated that one person in ten in the United Kingdom will enter hospital at some time in life with a predominantly psychological problem, and one in four will consult a doctor at some stage with such a condition. So there are relatively few people in the community today who will not directly or indirectly come in contact with emotional illness at some time. This may be in a friend, a relative, a workmate – or even in oneself. And, of course, there is a growing number of people, including social workers, ministers of religion, personnel officers and many others, who find themselves dealing with psychiatric problems as part of their professional work.

I believe that this book, and its companion volumes, will be of interest and value to all of them, from the professional, through the merely interested individual, to the sufferer and his relatives. It is not an alarmist book, it does not overstate its case and it conveys an impression of hopefulness which, in the 1970s, is a perfectly realistic and valid approach to adopt.

It illustrates by apposite case-examples and it makes no attempt to turn the reader into an amateur psychiatrist. Instead, it tries to alert him to certain phenomena which, if he learns to recognise them, may enable him to forestall much suffering and occasional tragedy.

The authors are both widely-experienced social workers and both have worked for long periods in the field of mental health. They have written this text on a topic they know well, but they have written it from a non-medical viewpoint. This gives them a freshness of insight into the problems raised by psychiatric illness and, I believe, an enhanced opportunity to communicate their knowledge to the lay public. Without tricks or mannerisms they are saying, 'This is how mental illness might present itself to *you*.' I have little doubt that the average reader will feel far more competent to take the first steps in dealing with a psychiatric problem after reading what they have to say.

Alistair Munro

Liverpool, 1974

Introduction

Mental illnesses have been suffered by man for as long as history itself and although the medical and allied professions have developed a considerable understanding of such illnesses – their genesis and treatment – the average man in the street has been left somewhat in the dark. This situation is exacerbated by the fact that doctors – particularly psychiatrists – have been invested by the public with something akin to magical qualities. This means that the public accept without question that which the doctor does, and where there are no questions, there can be no answers.

Physical illness can be comparatively easily understood and its effects discerned and sympathised with. Unfortunately, mental illness frequently produces apprehension in people. Unlike physical illness where the 'person' remains more or less intact in terms of his ability to communicate his feelings to those around him, the mentally ill person is seen to be a different 'person' – even to his relatives and friends. It seems that people can tolerate even the most mutilated living body because the personality remains intact. However, when the body appears to be healthy, but the 'person' changes, there is a lack of understanding of his condition which inevitably generates a corresponding lack of understanding of his behaviour towards others. When one learns to 'expect' how a person is likely to behave in most circumstances (i.e. to predict his behaviour), it is extremely perplexing when this expectation is met with strange or even bizarre behaviour. The closer people become emotionally, the more often their expectations are accurate. It therefore follows that the greater will be the perplexity when this no longer follows. It is fairly easy to understand physical accidents and ailments. A comparatively clear-cut cause-and-effect relationship is readily apparent which would explain the sick person's suffering – whether this be caused by a bus or a virus. This being so, it is even possible to allocate blame for the person's suffering. But, with psychiatrically ill people, there is no such clear-cut relationship between the illness and its cause; sometimes guilt is produced in those near and dear to the patient by their very efforts to explain the person's behaviour in terms which they can understand and accept. An alternative mode of reaction, on the part of family and friends, to the inexplicable behaviour produced by mental illness is to deny that there could be any external cause in which they were involved, or that such an illness could befall *them*. This in turn often means complete or partial rejection of the sufferer. Perhaps there is an understandable analogy to this to be found during war-time. It would be difficult for soldiers in action to dwell on the possibility that the next bullet was 'for them'. In order to keep sane and effective, they quickly develop a firm belief that death or injury is for others.

It is the authors' hope that this book will help to diminish the fears and anxieties so often associated with mental illness by providing realistic information, in lay terms, about the various manifestations of mental illness, its causes and its management. By doing this, it is our belief that understanding of, and compassion for, mentally sick people will be enhanced and, as a result, some of their suffering will be reduced. To aid understanding, we shall present pen-pictures of persons who are mentally ill, as we think they would appear to those in their immediate and wider environment, rather than as they might be seen by the specialists in the psychiatric field.

It is not our intention to create amateur psychiatrists, but only to provide sufficient information, so that understanding will result in sympathetic handling, a knowledge that help can be given and the form that such help might take. We are very conscious that 'a little learning is a dangerous thing' and we do not want to create new problems by encouraging the reader to become unduly introspective.

We hope that this book will be of interest and help, particularly to members of the public, because it is they who first come into contact with those who are psychiatrically sick.

Because it is our intention to present case material from the point of view of the public, we believe that this book will also be a valuable addition to the more traditional psychiatric literature which is produced for medical and social work students. Indeed, it is our sincere hope that the book will be of some use to everyone in the 'helping' professions – health visitors, teachers, nurses, the clergy, police, voluntary social workers and many others.

As we mentioned a little earlier in the introduction, we shall present a number of cases which illustrate the manifestations of psychiatric illnesses. These examples will then be developed, discussed and classified under the various descriptive headings used in psychiatry. The discussion will centre round the causes of mental illness and its management at two levels – in the immediate environment, and in professional settings. We shall, however, place more emphasis on the former, though we shall indicate also the proper use of professional services, which ensures that the patient receives the best possible attention while those around him may receive appropriate support.

We have chosen to approach the 'Social Problems associated with Psychiatric Illness' in the way that we have outlined because we, the authors, believe that it is a meaningful way for us, as social workers, to tackle the subject, and because this book is only one of a series which will cover at much greater depth the diagnostic categories of illness which we describe in outline.

authors' note
The cases which we will present throughout the book are based on real life situations known to the authors, but the material facts and the events portrayed have been deliberately altered, though without distortion of the essential truth. We have done this in order to emphasise cardinal points and also to ensure the complete anonymity of the people concerned.

1 Possession · containment · tolerance?

ancient times
In this chapter some account will be given of the history of the treatment of the mentally ill and of public attitudes that have influenced such treatment. There are available references to the treatment of persons we would describe today as mentally ill and of the manifestations of mental illness from very early times. An ancient Egyptian papyrus (*circa* 1500 BC) describes senility in the following brief, but accurate terms: 'The heart grows heavy and remembers not yesterday.' In this description we have two of the components of senile illness, namely the wasting physical process of old age, and the psychological component of memory loss. The 'shamans' (priests-cum-magicians) of early cultures used a process known as trephining (making small holes in the skull) to let out the devil spirits of those thought to be possessed. It is interesting to compare this ancient practice with the modern surgical treatment of some forms of mental disorder, in which fine probes are inserted in the frontal part of the skull. There are many references to the use of drugs for the treatment of mental illness in ancient times, for example Hellebore, which had been found useful in curing certain diseases in goats. The family too, was reminded of its responsibilities. Thus in Plato's *Republic*, we find the following comments. 'If anyone is insane, let him not be seen

openly in the city, but, let the relations of such a person watch over him in the best manner they know of, and if they are negligent, let them pay a fine.'

There are numerous references in the Bible to various aspects of behaviour associated with mental illness and to mental illness itself. For instance, there are six reported cases of actual or attempted suicide in the Old and New Testaments (three such examples being Saul, Ahitopel and Judas Iscariot).

Such behaviour was viewed with very mixed feelings. If indulged in on the battlefield to avoid capture, it was considered acceptable, but if indulged in for other reasons, the biblical commentators of the time seem to have been less generous. Thus, in the works of Josephus (first century AD) we find the statement – 'for those who have laid hands upon themselves, the darker regions of the netherworld receive their souls.'

The periodic illness of King Saul is often mentioned as being one of the first accounts we have of what would today be described as 'a depressive illness.' Thus, in the first book of Samuel, we find the statement – 'And when it came to pass, when the evil spirit from God was upon Saul, that David took his harp, and played with his hand; so Saul was refreshed and was well, and the evil spirit departed from him.' Though this is usually taken as an indication of depressive illness (and incidentally evidence of the early use of music as a form of therapy – a subject to which we will return later in this chapter), reference to Saul's illness in a later chapter of the Book of Samuel makes one wonder if it had some of the qualities of over-suspiciousness akin to what is today described as *paranoia* 'And it came to pass on the morrow, that the evil spirit from God came upon Saul . . . and David played with his hand as at other times, and there was a javelin in Saul's hand . . . and Saul cast the javelin; for he said, I will smite David even unto the wall with it . . .'

We read of King Nebuchadnezzer, wandering in his delirium, in which he believed himself to be changed into an animal – 'He did eat grass like an ox, and his body was wet with the dew of heaven, till his hairs grew like the feathers of eagles, and his nails like birds' claws.'

So much then for these brief biblical allusions. We must now turn to the contributions of some of the early men of medicine. Of these, Hippocrates (*circa* 460 BC) is important, in that he made a special contribution to the study of psychological disorders. There were three main aspects of his work in this field. First, he recognised the importance of the brain as an organ of mind. Secondly, he sought a more rational (that is, physiological) explanation of the various temperaments, moods and emotional disorders he encountered in his patients, and endeavoured to make connections between physiological and psychological relationships. Thirdly, he attacked vigorously the conception of divinely ordained, *and therefore unalterable* illness. A good example of this was epilepsy, which was known for long as the 'sacred' disease. 'You will see,' he said, 'on examination of the brains of epileptic patients – that it is not God which injures the body but disease.' Needless to say, his teachings which tried to rescue medicine from the arena of mysticism were not at all well received (D. Stafford Clark). A number of other early physicians also made important contributions to the study of mental illness. Aesclepiades was a very shrewd clinical observer, and was, for his time, humane. He recommended music as a form of sedation (see above also), warm baths, soft hammocks and light. 'Patients should be kept in well-lighted places; darkness leads to terror, and terror increases the misery of madness.'

Celsus was what we would describe today as a medical journalist. It is of interest to note how many of these early workers in the field of mental disorder appear to have been 'laymen' and not strictly physicians as then known. Perhaps they were the precursors of modern developments in psychiatry, in which laymen (in the sense of not being medical personnel) have been increasingly involved. Celsus wrote of the manic patient: 'When he has said or done anything wrong, he must be chastised by hunger, chains and fetters . . . it is also beneficial in this malady to make use of sudden fright, for a change may be effected by withdrawing the mind from the state in which it has been . . .' The intention may appear laudable, but the methods used seem to have been barbaric. Some people consider certain of the modern forms of psychiatric treatment in much the same light, as for example, treatment by electro-convulsive therapy; but the comparison is not really tenable and is only made here to show some historical connections. Aretaeus of Cappadocia was probably the first physician to consider the idea of spontaneous remission of psychiatric illness, and Soranus, the Greco-Roman physician (2nd century A.D.), attacked the barbarity of contemporary forms of treatment, stressing, as had Aesclepiades much earlier, the need for therapy and an approach that discriminated according to individual need. Much of his work comes to us through his chronicler Caelius Aurelianus. However, Caelius could not share Soranus's toleration of what we would now call the sexual perversions. In his book entitled *De Incubone*, he gave his own authority to the existing view that a special kind of demon existed which could enter the souls of women (and men for that matter) and possess them for sexual purposes.

These attitudes reflected what was probably the beginning of the shadow of demonology – a shadow which was to hang over the treatment of the insane for the next sixteen hundred years. However, before considering this period in more detail, brief mention must be made of the work of the physician Galen of Pergamum (2nd century A.D.). Galen tried to encourage a return to the use of clinical observation as first advanced by Hippocrates. He stressed the dependence of the personality on physical health and advanced a rather ambitious connection between brain substance and mental performance. 'The keenness of the mind depends upon the firmness of the brain substance. Slow thinking is due to heaviness . . . its firmness and stability produces the faculty of memory . . .' In statements such as these we have glimmerings of the later science of neurology – a sister science of much importance to psychiatry. The 'dark ages' in psychiatry can be said to begin with the death of Galen.

demonology: The period of demonology dates from about AD 200 and existed until the latter part of the eighteenth century. During these long ages, theologians were able to use biblical allusions to the mentally afflicted, to search out and eliminate those who were different and were thought to be 'possessed' – those of whom they were afraid. Thus, they could refer to exhortations such as in Exodus: 'Thou shalt not suffer a witch to live,' and in Leviticus: 'A man, also a woman, that hath a familiar spirit or that is a wizard shall be put to death.' (The theologians had obviously not chosen to remember that Christ had 'cast out devils.')

There then ensued various manoeuvres to exorcise consort with the 'power of evil', by charms and prayers. Such exorcisms were used in an attempt to cure all kinds of disturbances, such as that now described as hysteria, for example. This was a malady long believed to be due to the wandering of the womb about the body. When these attempts failed, other and more brutal methods were resorted to. The first 'witch' was formally executed in about AD 430. They were soon to be executed in their thousands. In Geneva, some five hundred were burned in three months in 1515. Before the Reformation, the principal authority for such 'witch-hunting' practices was a work written by two monks called Kramer and Sprenger and entitled the 'Malleus Malificarum' (or 'Witches' Hammer'). One part of this terrifying book deals with the recognition of phenomena we now consider to be associated with certain forms of psychiatric illness (for example, anaesthetic areas of the skin, which can be increased or decreased at the suggestion of the examiner. Today we would describe this as an hysterical manifestation.) The sections in the 'Malleus' on the examination of suspects, and the physical extraction of confessions, bear comparison with the methods used by the Gestapo in the Second World War, and with the more recent accounts of the methods employed towards political prisoners in some countries.

After the Reformation, things if anything became worse, because it is said the Protestants vied in zeal with the Catholics in destroying those 'possessed of Devils.' Even so distinguished a physician as Paré (the father of modern surgery) believed that the only proper treatment for a man claiming magical powers was execution. However, there were some people holding more moderate views at this time of persecution and oppression. Paracelsus considered that 'mental diseases (had) nothing to do with evil spirits or devils . . . one should not study how to exorcise the devil, but rather how to cure the insane.' His contemporary, Vives, published many works which contested the whole basis of the 'Malleus Malificarum' and Johann Weyer, another fearless denunciator of persecution, made a considerable contribution to the beginnings of an attempt to classify mental conditions. He was much in conflict with the Inquisition, of which he said: 'It is highly unpleasant to see how people, in order to kill errors, are busy killing human beings.' (It is sad to relate that some hundred years after his death, nineteen people were executed and one tortured to death, in the famous Salem witch hunt of 1691–2.)

summary of attitudes in the middle ages

It is important to remember that, from a caring point of view, the village was in fact the 'total institution' for most people and that (more importantly) the last word on any subject rested with the Church as arbiter. The provision of hospitals was the Church's duty; psychological disorders became part of demonology, therefore coming within the aegis of the Clergy. It has also been suggested that the Black Death left physically and emotionally exhausted nations, prone to outbursts of neurotic illness. These have been well described by writers of those times.

the seventeenth century

The seventeenth century was characterised by what we would today describe as a 'knowledge explosion' in many fields, particularly in areas that were relevant to medicine. Three examples may be given. Firstly, the discovery of the mechanics of the circulation of the blood. Secondly, the invention and development of the microscope. Thirdly, the development of Newtonian physics. It was, of course, also the age of philosophical discovery and controversy. Despite these developments, not much attention was directed specifically towards mental illness at this time, but Felix Plater was a notable exception; he added to previous work on classification.

Despite advances in science and philosophy, fairly primitive ideas remained, as can be seen in the following examples. Willis, a famous anatomist, suggested of mental treatment that 'the primary object is naturally curative; discipline, threats and blows are needed as much as medical treatment . . .' Blood-letting was also common at this time (frequently until death intervened). This was eventually supplanted by crude attempts at blood *transfusion* in which the blood of young, sane men was transfused into the blood of the aged insane. Not surprisingly, it was a complete failure. Some of the medicines prescribed at this time make for fascinating, if somewhat unpalatable, reading. Thus Sydenham – a very famous physician – prescribed for mania a concoction known as 'Venice treacle'. This contained the flesh and blood of vipers and sixty-one other ingredients, including canary wine and honey.

the eighteenth century

In the eighteenth century, an important principle was gradually recognised, namely, that the forces of mind and body interacted (this principle had been suggested by Hippocrates many centuries earlier). The re-establishment of this principle owed much to the work of George Stahl, a German professor of medicine. Yet, tragically enough, alongside these newer ideas and their far-reaching implications, there existed attitudes that we find hard to comprehend today. Thus, even forward-looking workers like Brown in this country, Rush in America and Reil in Germany, could all recommend treatments that we would consider barbaric; Reil used 'non-injurious torture' – flinging patients into water, firing cannons, and confronting them with visions of those risen from the dead. Those interested in art will recognise the graphic presentations of various forms of mental illness in the paintings of Hogarth, particularly the 'Rake's Progress'.

Attention was focused increasingly on the problems of the mentally ill through the thirty year intermittent illness of George III (the diagnosis of which has always been in some doubt). Even as a royal patient, however, he received no special favours. One attendant boasted that he had knocked the King 'as flat as a flounder.'

The treatment provided for the mentally ill in the eighteenth century can be summarised in the following fashion (and in so summarising them, we should note that they were treatment provisions still based largely on superstition, moral condemnation, ignorance and apathy). There were patients:
(1) Confined under the Poor Laws.
(2) Confined under the Criminal Law.
(3) Confined under the Vagrancy Laws.
(4) Confined in private madhouses.
(5) Confined as Bethlem (Bedlam) Patients.
(6) Confined as 'single lunatics' (that is, confined alone in various places, under the most appalling conditions) (Jones, 1972).

Public concern about these provisions grew stronger towards the end of the century. This concern resulted in various enquiries and subsequent legislation 'for the better regulation of private madhouses'. An interesting feature of the late eighteenth century was the apparently high proportion of famous literary people said to suffer from some form of mental illness. (Examples are Cowper, Dr Johnson, Oliver Goldsmith, William Collins, Blake, and the sister of Charles Lamb.) Their plight may also have encouraged this developing public concern.

The history of the treatment of the insane from earliest times up to the end of the eighteenth century is mainly characterised by fear of those who were 'possessed'. There were, however, occasional instances of humane treatment and attempts to understand symptoms. As the nineteenth century began, there developed a preoccupation with 'containment'; the latter part of this chapter deals with this preoccupation and the movement towards a greater degree of toleration and understanding of the mentally ill.

In the nineteenth and twentieth centuries, according to Henderson and Gillespie, four main areas of development are to be discerned in the treatment of the mentally ill, though these overlap very considerably.
(1) The period of humane reform.
(2) The introduction of non-restraint.

(3) The hospital period.
(4) The social and community period.

These will now be discussed in turn.

(1) the period of humane reform

The movement for humane reform occurred in this country and on the Continent of Europe. Two of its most prominent leaders were the Frenchmen, Pinel and Esquirol; they are usually regarded as the pioneers of 'moral treatment' of the insane – that is, the abolition of restraints and of the more violent forms of treatment. In this country, the foundation of the 'Retreat' at York by William Tuke and the Royal Edinburgh Hospital by Andrew Duncan, reflect comparable developments. As has already been mentioned, public interest in 'madhouses' and the care of the insane was growing. Lunacy law in England has its origins as far back as an Act of 1320, which dealt largely with the property of lunatics. However, it was not until the beginning of the nineteenth century that we see introduced a spate of legislation to deal with the more general *care and control* of the mentally disordered. In 1815, a Commission was set up to 'consider provision being made for the better regulation of madhouses in England.' Some of the matters revealed by that Commission make horrifying reading. Those wishing to obtain more details of the conditions that existed at the time will find pages 41–44 of David Stafford Clark's book *Psychiatry Today* (Second Ed. 1963) unpleasant, but rewarding, reading. Lest we become too complacent about these past events, we should note that a number of very recent enquiries into conditions in some modern psychiatric hospitals have revealed a state of affairs of which the whole community should feel ashamed. (For one example see *Report of the Committee of Enquiry into Whittingham Hospital:* Cmnd. 4861, Feb. 1972; especially paras. 34–37 and para. 107.)

By about 1845, some attempt had been made to exercise control over what had been the worst abuses. A national inspectorate had been achieved, and institutions of all types gradually came under supervision. Between 1845 and 1890, county asylums became the basis for the new system – the driving force behind this being Ashley, 7th Earl of Shaftesbury.

the lunacy act of 1890: This has been described, correctly, as a 'monument to legalism' in its massive construction of legal powers and controls. This Act codified all previous legislation. It was much concerned with the protection of patients from *unlawful containment and private vengeance*. Such protection was necessary at this time largely because of the inadequacies of medical training and skill in the field of mental illness. Conversely, it also aimed at protecting doctors from 'vexatious litigants.'

Brief mention must be made here of the problem of mental deficiency. It was not until 1845 that (in practice) separate treatment for the mentally defective was introduced. A permissive act for State Aid for mental deficiency hospitals was passed in 1886. Some time later a Royal Commission was appointed as a result of the growing concern about the growing problem of 'feeble-mindedness' and associated disorders of behaviour. This reported in 1908, stressing the poverty of provisions to deal with the situation and their lack of uniformity. By the Mental Deficiency Act of 1913, control was vested in the newly established Board of Control (replacing the earlier Lunacy Commission). This newly established central body was to be responsible for *all* types of mental care.

psychiatry in the nineteenth century: Doctors studying the treatment of the mentally ill were becoming interested in the problems of the less frankly 'mad' and concentrating their attentions upon what we would regard today as the 'neuroses'. This interest began with the work of Anton Mesmer (Mesmerism, a form of hypnosis, is named after him), and later by Charcot, Janet and Freud. It should be noted that, although Freud is the father of psychoanalysis, he was primarily a medical scientist – a neurologist. In this country, Henry Maudsley (after whom the Maudsley Hospital is named) stressed the importance of the body-mind relationship once again (thus forging interesting historical links with Hippocrates and George Stahl). In the nineteen-twenties, this relationship was to be taken further by Adolf Meyer with his school of 'psycho-biology'. In the field of the more frankly 'mad', the names of Kraepelin and Bleuler should be mentioned, since they made important contributions to refining the classifications of mental illnesses.

Child psychiatry had its origins at about this time, too, through the work of child health physicians (paediatricians) such as Bakwin and Cameron (whose book *The Nervous Child* had a considerable impact). A significant later contribution to the field of child psychiatry in particular, and to attitudes towards childhood misconduct and delinquency in general, was to be made in the nineteen-twenties by the late Sir Cyril Burt in his studies of delinquent and mentally-retarded children. Burt's work characterised a developing trend towards trying to *understand* wayward children and young people instead of labelling them merely as 'naughty' and misbehaved.

The development of adult psychiatry in the late nineteenth century was also facilitated by discoveries in the field of organic pathology. It seems necessary to stress this, because the relevance of physical factors in the causation of mental disorder is sometimes underestimated. Kraft-Ebbing, who is usually best remembered for his writings on sexual perversion, paved the way for the discovery of the syphilitic origins of the psychiatric disorder known as 'general paralysis of the insane' (G.P.I.). This demonstrated clearly an organic basis for an apparently psychologically-determined disease.

patterns of mental illness at different historical periods
So far, nothing has been said about the prevalence of psychiatric disorders at different periods in history. It is of course impossible to make precise calculations. Reference has already been made to what appears to have been a prevalence of neurotic disorder following the Black Death. At that time, malnutrition would also be common, showing itself in conditions such as pellagra, which have psychiatric after-effects.

Life expectancy being short, the psychiatric disorders of old age would be uncommon, though steadily increasing with the population explosion of the late nineteenth century. Specific diseases such as G.P.I. (referred to above) were probably fairly uncommon in the middle ages, increasing considerably in frequency after the Napoleonic Wars, as a result of the spread of venereal disease. Although many people assert that there has been a marked increase in the prevalence of various psychiatric disorders, it is difficult to state with any certainty whether this is an *actual* or an *apparent* increase. The pace of modern life and the strains of such living are often quoted in support of an alleged increase in psychiatric disorders, but the evidence is not conclusive and we can only make rather vague assumptions. One would have to make allowance for such things as population increases, the better recognition of some disorders and more readily available treatment facilities.

(2) the period of non-restraint

During the middle of the nineteenth century, methods of mechanical restraint were gradually abolished. As a result, patients actually became more easy to control and accidents and suicides decreased. Connolly, at Hanwell Asylum (now St Bernard's Hospital, Southall in Middlesex), was a notable advocate of this approach. In the U.S.A., the movement towards non-restraint was led by a remarkable woman pioneer, Dorothea Lynde Dix. For health reasons, she settled in Scotland and by her determination, succeeded in putting right abuses that others had been struggling for years to correct. During this period, there also developed the 'colony' concept – notably on the Continent, the colony at Gheel, in Belgium, being the most famous. There is an interesting legend connected with the foundation of this colony. It is said that Dymphna – the daughter of an Irish king – had fled to Gheel because of her father's incestuous advances towards her. He eventually captured and then beheaded her. It is said that her death was witnessed by some mentally afflicted persons, who were said to have immediately recovered their sanity. Subsequently the place became one of pilgrimage and the colony was later founded as a result. In more recent years, it has provided a central psychiatric hospital and also facilities for large numbers of patients to live in private homes under foster care, thus forging helpful links with the community.

(3) the hospital period

Following the period of 'non-restraint', came a period of

'seclusion'. (There are interesting near-parallels here with the movement for seclusion in the history of our prisons.) The same period saw the introduction of female nurses into male wards (in about the eighteen-forties). This was followed by better training for nursing staff and the promotion of some to positions as matrons in some psychiatric hospitals. Gradually, smaller ward units were introduced. In the last twenty years or so, the medical superintendent has been replaced in many instances by a chairman of a board of consultants. Some people regret the passing of the direct control of the hospital by one person, in the role of the medical superintendent, and consider that it may have led to abuse and neglect of patients. This is a matter of some controversy, but it is noteworthy that Scotland has decided to retain the post of Medical Superintendent in its psychiatric hospitals.

Experiments have also been undertaken in the provision of Day and Night Hospitals, and in the last thirty years or so there has been a considerable increase in the amount of psychiatry taught to medical students. Undergraduate training for adult psychiatry has been firmly established, but regrettably, the same cannot be said of the child psychiatric field, nor of mental handicap.

Reference has already been made to the Mental Deficiency Act of 1913. This was a further (though largely legal and administrative) attempt at classification, aimed at separating the treatment of imbeciles and defectives (as they were then called) from the mentally disordered. During the nineteen-twenties and thirties, various new medical procedures were introduced, such as physical treatments for depression and schizophrenia, the use of more modern drugs and psycho-surgery. Opinions have always been divided as to the efficacy and ethics of the use of some of these methods. The Mental Treatment Act of 1930 made it possible, for the first time, for treatment to be provided on a voluntary basis, though such treatment had already been provided unofficially by the Maudsley Hospital, some fifteen years earlier.

Attention was focused again on the question of mental deficiency in the nineteen-thirties. It is possible that at this time there was more public sympathy with this group because they were considered as 'weaker brethren' who were less fear-provoking than the insane. The Mental Deficiency Act of 1927 made a minor, but very important amendment to previous legislation. It made specific reference to the 'acquisition', as opposed to the 'inheritance', of mental defect, caused for example as a result of disease or injury *after* the earliest years. This amendment was made necessary largely as a result of an outbreak of epidemic *encephalitis lethargica* in the nineteen-twenties, one of the effects of this illness being mental retardation. A Government Committee (the Wood Committee) reporting in 1929, stressed the need for better institutional care for mentally defective persons, and the encouragement of more positive attitudes towards them by the community. It also recommended further efforts to distinguish between 'primary' (i.e. genetically acquired) mental deficiency and its 'secondary' forms (i.e. acquired as a result of injury or disease).

During the late nineteen-thirties, increasing interest was also shown in the relationship between crime and less severe forms of mental disorder and the Criminal Justice Act of 1948 enabled courts to make mental treatment (as an in- or out-patient) a formal condition of probation.

(4) the movement towards community psychiatry

Five influences seem to have been at work which have contributed towards the development of what is known as *community psychiatry*.

Firstly, a developing interest in the effects of the social environment upon the individual. The work of the early child guidance clinics, already referred to, is of importance here, concentrating as it did upon the formative influence of home and family.

Secondly, the use of physical and other methods of psychiatric treatment meant that a higher proportion of patients could be returned to the community more quickly.

Thirdly, there was a developing awareness of the problems of the mentally disordered by the medical profession. This came about largely as the result of the improvements and experiments in medical education previously mentioned.

Fourthly, evidence from the work of various authorities (such as John Bowlby) who had examined some of the harmful effects of prolonged institutional care.

Fifthly, a developing awareness on the part of the general public of the problems of mental illness. In part, this had developed out of the 'Mental Hygiene Movement.' This movement, American in origin, owed much to the influence of a man called Clifford Beers, who had written an autobiographical account of his experiences as a mental patient. In this country, the work of the National Association for Mental Health has been of great significance. This organisation was formed in the late 1940s from four independent associations that over the years had been influential in the mental health field. These were the Mental After-Care Association, the Central Association for Mental Welfare, the National Council for Mental Hygiene and the Child Guidance Council. The N.A.M.H., or MIND as it is now commonly known, seeks to promote knowledge about mental disorder and to provide public, as well as professional, education in this field.

the last fifteen years: The last fifteen years or so have been characterised by a number of trends and developments. These can be summarised as follows:

Firstly, problems of mental illness should now be seen as comparable with those of other illnesses; to this end, treatment should be part of other health and welfare provisions. This principle was accepted (at least in theory) in the passing of the Mental Health Act, 1959. It is true to say, however, that sufficient resources have never been available to meet the lofty principles enshrined in this forward-looking piece of legislation, although encouraging developments are now afoot.

Secondly, though certain limited safeguards might seem to be necessary, the whole machinery of judicial and administrative intervention in the field of mental disorder, appropriate to the nineteenth century, could largely be done away with. It is interesting to note that the main impetus for this change came from the Board of Control itself.

Thirdly, the legal distinctions between mental deficiency

and mental disorder were no longer considered necessary; both types of condition could be dealt with under one enactment, thus changing the 'separatism' that had been reintroduced by the Act of 1913.

Fourthly, treatment should be on an informal basis wherever possible.

Fifthly, the powers of control and inspection previously invested in the Board of Control were vested in the Ministry (now the Department) of Health. Some people consider that this has been much to the disadvantage of psychiatric patients. Hitherto, there was one recognised independent department of central government concerned with their interests. People fear that these interests may now tend to be overlooked. This may explain the recently expressed need for continued inspection of psychiatric and subnormality hospitals and a psychiatric hospital 'Ombudsman.'

Sixthly, a number of experiments have been undertaken using new modes of patient 'management.' These are aimed at involving the patient more actively in self-therapy and at using the whole community as 'therapist.' This approach had its origins during the Second World War and was probably influenced to a large degree by the earlier approaches to treatment practised in the U.S.A. and on the Continent by such workers as Moreno and Aichorn. The replacement of medical superintendents by committees of consultants has been accompanied by the increasing appearance of lay administrators. Treatment of the mentally ill is becoming less and less the exclusive prerogative of the medical profession (a return to earlier times perhaps). This development could well go some way not only to removing the 'magic' and fear of psychiatry, but also towards making it more comprehensible to the public at large.

summary

Generally speaking, the nineteenth and twentieth centuries can be said to be marked by an increasingly more humane and rational approach to the mentally ill. Methods of treatment and containment are now less primitive, though as has already been indicated, recent enquiries have shown a greater degree of barbarity than some would have thought possible in this day and age. We have moved through periods when we talked of 'madmen' or of 'lunatics' and 'idiots' (or 'simple fools') to the time when we spoke of the insane,' and more recently of the 'mentally ill'. The degree to which we have really become more tolerant (readers will have noticed the question mark after the word 'Tolerance' in the title of this chapter) is very much an open question. Those people who have been concerned with attempts to rehabilitate a mentally ill or a subnormal patient, or to deal with the anxieties of residents in an area where the authorities are attempting to establish a psychiatric hostel, will know that some of the attitudes described in this chapter (particularly in the first part) are still very prevalent. Such attitudes seem to defy rational attempts at resolution. However, one thing is certain; continued attempts must be made to 'lower the temperature' in this field, so that the public loses its fear of those who are mentally ill. Accurate information and education can go some way to help in this direction; this is perhaps the most important reason for writing this book.

references

This chapter draws heavily upon the following three sources to which grateful acknowledgement is made and which should be consulted for further reference:

Stafford Clark, D. *Psychiatry Today* (2nd Ed.). Penguin Books. Harmondsworth, 1963.

Henderson, D., and Batchelor, I. R. C. Henderson and Gillespie's *Textbook of Psychiatry*. Oxford University Press. 1962. (*Chapter I.*)

Jones, K. *A History of the Mental Health Services*. Routledge. London, 1971.

2 Mental health and mental illness

In this modern world, people have become more concerned to think in terms of the prevention of mental illness than at any time in the past. Obviously, this is a desirable progression, but because this more positive thinking about mental illness has only just begun to be implemented by action, there is a possibility that the public may be confused by references to 'mental health' when, from their point of view, the various services appear to be, and are, caring for the mentally 'sick.' It is hardly surprising that, when a section in a local authority health or welfare department is called 'Department of Mental Health' but is known to deal mainly with mental illness, the general public will continue to project many of the old stigmata to the new department. Indeed, even in high places, this confusion persists to such an extent that during a recent Mental Health campaign, a member of a local health committee in a television plea for public support, said that there was a need for greater attention to be paid to *mental health*, because, 'there are far more people suffering from this complaint than is generally imagined'! Of course, she meant mental illness, but her misapprehension did nothing to clear the general confusion.

Since it is the present authors' intention to present, in simple terms, the social aspects of *psychiatric disorder* (*mental ill health*) so that there will be a better understanding of the behaviour of people in their environment, we would like to begin by outlining what we believe mental health to be. By so doing, it is hoped that the reader will be better and more quickly able to observe when friends or relatives are moving from this state towards illness and, conversely, to help them to assess when people, who are sick, are on the mend. It is also hoped that, by indicating how the healthy person conducts his life, the reader will be more capable of understanding measures which can be taken to prevent the occurrence of psychiatric disorders (when this is possible). Although, thus far, we have used the terms *psychiatric disorder* and *mental illness* interchangeably, it is our intention from this point onwards to use the term *psychiatric disorder* exclusively. We do this because one of our main aims – as stated in the introduction to our book – is to reduce those fears which tend to be associated with the word '*mental*,' even when the main emphasis on the word is a healthy one. To emphasise this point, an example springs to mind. Some time ago, in an adoption agency, after the usual initial assessment procedures, a young couple were considered to have the makings of ideal parents. When a baby became available for them, they were told that the child concerned was the daughter of a 'mental nurse.' The social worker became aware of a cooling in interest, which was only put right when she explained that, by mental nurse, she meant a nurse who worked in a mental hospital.

According to Karl Menninger (in Jahoda, 1958), the term 'mental health' is defined as 'the adjustment of human beings to the world and to each other with a maximum of effectiveness and happiness; not just efficiency, or just contentment, or the grace of obeying the rules of the game cheerfully, but all of these together. It is the ability to maintain an even temper, and an alert intelligence, socially considerate behaviour, and a happy disposition.' This, according to Menninger, epitomises the healthy mind. This definition would seem to be very much in accord with the stand we are adopting in this book and in particular, that part which deals with socially considerate behaviour. It is the authors' hope that if such a state of psychological equilibrium could be more commonly achieved, there would be a marked diminution in psychiatric disorders.

Mental health also involves maturity – a process of growing up, rather than of simply growing older. It involves integrity of the personality which has accommodated to the conflict of having to play different parts (roles) in life. People and loving interpersonal relationships are essential, as is a form of security – not necessarily material security – which allows people to develop or grow by the experience of decision-making. In other words, mental health is a process which is involved with learning, at all stages in life. According to Professor Langeveld (1970), this learning is 'the total process of up-bringing from birth to maturity, with a predominant stress on a child's most direct relatives; the parents, the home, the conditions of a cultural and personal kind prevailing in that relationship . . .' Langeveld pointed out that mental health and maturity were inevitably intertwined and he suggested that there were six criteria against which mental health could be measured:

(1) *Responsibility:* When Langeveld referred to this aspect, he was not thinking about morality but of the inevitable demands of life. Present attitudes are still very much concerned with morality and, of course, in contemporary society this is seen as a restrictive stand to take and this must be recognised. People should be made acutely aware that there is room for failure, as well as for success; that one suffers the consequences of one's own actions; that responsibility has to be shared with others and that we all have responsibility *for* the weak and the helpless.

(2) *Competence and willingness to carry out tasks:* By behaving in a responsible way, one becomes *competent*, and this enables us to lead a life which is both productive and harmonious. It also permits us to carry out those tasks for which we are best suited, in such a way that we help society rather than kick against it.

(3) *Self-correction:* This aspect must become increasingly developed in the pursuit of satisfaction and this is usually

accomplished by experiencing approval for our achievements.

(4) *Self-knowledge:* With each satisfying success, there comes a realisation that new possibilities exist for us, both externally and internally. To achieve this involves learning about the world and one's position in it from failure, providing that we can see that failure, and self-knowledge from failures, are not peculiar to *us*.

(5) *Commonsense:* This aspect is immediately apparent when our limitations are known; when the willingness to accept information or guidance is developed; and where there is a recognition of our inner resistances.

(6) *Self-reliance:* This, according to Langeveld, has been achieved when, along with the previous criteria, we have learned to commit ourselves to others, while at the same time retaining our own identity. This is the ability to stand on one's own feet.

Growth in the ability to care for others – for strangers as well as for friends or family – is what we are aiming at in this book. We appreciate that this may be a difficult task, since it is not something that can be done by offering direct advice. Broadly, our aim is to provide sufficient information to enable the reader to recognise what is involved in mental illness. Leona Tyler (1970), in talking about the smooth functioning of our highly complex society, which operates without many rigid social controls, has said that there are two main aspects of helping: 'the first is a sorting function. Individuals differ from one another in innumerable ways . . . size, shape, strength, talents, interests, motives. Society needs a variety of people to play different specialised roles. What must be accomplished is to match the persons to the demands . . . helping people find places in which each can contribute to society in his own special way. The second contribution is helping society to maintain its members in the kind of mental and emotional state that will enable them to carry out their responsibilities . . . This contribution (the mental health one) is often expressed only in terms of the happiness and welfare of individuals, but it obviously has to do also with the smooth running of society as a whole. Just as the most delicate machine requires oil to keep its parts from abrading each other, a delicately balanced, complex, social order must have some means for reducing abrasiveness between its parts and maintaining each part in good working order.'

Society is made up of major and minor groupings – from the largest, the State, at the top, through various organisations, cultural, political or social groupings, to our home, school or work groups, which are more intimately related to us. We have to learn to adjust, and to enable other people to adjust, to the multitude of varied experiences they encounter with other individuals. Each of these experiences can cause stress, if adjustment is either inadequate or impossible, because of the host of varied and often conflicting standards that society sets for its members. Often, the rules for playing the roles which are demanded of us are incomplete or ambiguous, and when this is so, horizons can only be widened by making the rules more explicit. We believe that the only way we can diminish stress among those around us (e.g., friends, neighbours, relatives, workmates etc.) is to help them to be emotionally satisfied to live in society, for society so often changes its norms and values faster than its members can adjust to them – it is then inevitable that for some, tension, if not mental illness, will result. According to Scott (in Sarbin, 1967), a serious obstacle to the understanding of mental illness lies in the lack of a clear definition of the term. 'The term "mental ill health" has been used by different researchers to refer to such diverse manifestations as schizophrenia, suicide, unhappiness, juvenile delinquency and passive acceptance of an intolerable environment. Whether some or all of these various reactions should be included in a single category of "mental illness" is not clear from a survey of the current literature.'

Difficult though it may be to define what is meant by mental ill health, what is important is that the reader is aware of our standpoint. What we mean in this book when we refer to psychiatric disorder is, that people who suffer from such illness are frequently unable, for psychological reasons, to fulfil their lives to their own satisfaction. Alternatively, they are so disturbed, that they require some form of psychiatric or social help. We do not want to enter into a lengthy discussion in order to arrive at a definition which could be universally acceptable. When we say 'so disturbed' this is a relative term; in other words, some people can be contained within, and supported by, their own social environment, while others require specialist help outside of it. It follows from our very loose definition that there may be as many psychiatrically disturbed people who never come into contact with helping agencies as there are who do. *In sum, we are attempting to draw the reader's attention to people who need help.*

In discussing mental health, we have tried to indicate the characteristics of the healthy state, and in order to understand how this develops we must now say something about the normal developmental processes which appear to be associated with health. We are deliberately avoiding the use of the term 'normality' – since what may be normal for one person may not be for another. There is no gainsaying the fact that every person is unique. Nevertheless, from birth to death there are certain processes which are common to the average man and woman.

In these developmental processes certain *crises* have to be met. If resolved successfully, the solutions can be used as a springboard to meet the crises which follow. In Langeveld's terms, which we have just outlined, it can be said that, with the satisfaction which comes from successfully resolving problems or crises, we realise that our possibilities for further experience are the greater. Life crises begin with birth and are usually followed by crisis situations at identifiable stages later in life – going to school, changing school, changing home, educational achievement, puberty and adolescence, courtship, marriage, parenthood, work, mid-life crises, bereavements, illnesses, retiral, and preparation for death. These are crisis situations for most of us. When these crises situations arise in childhood, we are helped through them by the adults around us who, according to Langeveld, act as the bridge between 'the one-time child and the self-reliant adult.' Langeveld maintained that the totality of living from birth to death was an educational one – that it was a total process of upbringing to complete maturity, with a predominant emphasis in the first place on the child's most intimate environment; the parents, the home and the conditions of a cultural and personal kind which prevail in these relationships.

This is put rather nicely in the Report of the *Underwood Committee* (1955), when it is stated that 'the first act of the drama in a child's struggle for independence is normally played out within the family, and in it the mother normally takes the leading role, since it is she who makes the first essay at independence possible and it is from her that he must first detach himself.' Most writers are agreed that the period of *infancy* – the first seven years – is the one in which support and approval of adults are most vital. The importance of this period, according to the Underwood Report, is that 'the world is presented to him, right from the beginning, as predominantly good or bad according to the quality of the mothering he receives. He needs one person constantly with him, not only to feed, care for and love him, but also to allow him to enjoy this relationship. In this way, he builds up the sense of security which he needs if he is to reach out, or respond, to other people sufficiently to commit himself and run the risk of getting hurt; and it is not until a person has the confidence to take this risk that he can fully give or receive affection.' But, even with warmth and security, the problems we have referred to still arise. For example, round about the age of three, there is still some uncertainty as to the friendliness or otherwise of the child's world, and this uncertainty not infrequently produces some difficult behaviour. Because these are formative years, the handling he receives at this time will shape the child's ability to accept frustration in later years. Fortunately, also at about this time, the father assumes a more important role as the representative of authority and the protector of the family.

According to the Underwood Report, 'if the period of conflict with authority is brought to a satisfactory conclusion, a child normally enters on a much calmer phase, greatly helped in this progress towards independence by the development of a genuine desire for friendship with other children.' Since this stage is reached at or about the child's fifth year, it can readily be seen that he has been prepared to meet one of the major crises – separation from mother by going to school. From this point onwards the child's world expands; teachers, other adults, school friends, all enter into his orbit. And so the process continues. There is no doubt that whether a child is happy and stable during later childhood, depends largely on his experiences during the earlier stage.

During this later period, the child's interests develop and widen and all this time he is monitoring these life-events and, given the experience of early security and warmth, his mind and feelings expand in harmony with his environment. But, as in the earlier period, one of the most important factors is a good relationship with parents. According to the Underwood Report, in the pre-adolescent stage 'a child's life and interests are no longer entirely centred on his home and his school. He may join other groups where he will meet adults in a rather different guise . . . in a freer and more friendly atmosphere than is usually possible at school. His passion for experimentation, his desire for independence, or the influence of other children, may occasionally lead him to lie, cheat or pilfer, but, by the end of the period, he has normally developed considerable resistance to temptation and is reliable, cheerful and co-operative . . .'

With adolescence, a particularly difficult period approaches and there are many choices which can be made in the striving to become a mature adult. But, providing that the adolescent can be helped to face the consequences of his own actions, whether these be related to success or to failure, the crises met in this period have an obvious value in the development of personality in general and of self-correction in particular. This important period is, characteristically, a period of indecision; a period of adjustment and readjustment; a period of experimentation; a period of rebellion; a period of great fluctuations in behaviour and in mood – sometimes angry, sometimes placid, sometimes rebellious, sometimes obedient, sometimes kind and sometimes cruel. It is a period when extremes of behaviour tend to occur with confusing rapidity. One can identify behaviour during adolescence which, if it were to persist, could be regarded as 'sick behaviour' and this is true of both passive and aggressive aspects of behaviour. This makes it difficult on occasion to determine to what extent the conduct observed at any one time is within the bounds of acceptability or is psychologically abnormal. The decision about this frequently depends on the mental attitudes of the observer himself, and how much experience he has had with adolescents.

In non-professional intervention, decisions are usually made by interpreting observed behaviour and just at this crucial point of development, when the adolescent must make his own *satisfying* decisions in order to develop in a healthy manner, any misinterpretation can have devastating results which may go on to produce a chain reaction. As we have indicated, during adolescence much is learned by experimentation in the drive to become an adult and when an observer wrongly interprets an isolated piece of behaviour, this in turn often provokes inappropriate responses. These heighten the barrier to understanding between the adolescent and this adult and, therefore, all adults, and the adolescent will inevitably experience further difficulties during this problem transition period. Too often, we profess that we understand how difficult it is to grow up and we say piously that youngsters need help in the process. We then go on to advise, cajole, and coerce them to see reason by 'doing it my way'. We do not look ahead *with* young people, we do it *for* them, without bothering to find out just what decisions we take on their behalf really mean to *them*. In other words, healthy development during this critical period involves helping youngsters to make their own decisions and thereby to get satisfaction from so doing.

The process of adjustment, in relation to the crises already mentioned, tends to occur in fairly clear-cut periods of life in adulthood, in courtship, in marriage, in parenthood, in midlife and in old age. We have concentrated on the early periods because we hope it has become apparent to the reader that the importance of these periods can establish the ability to handle the other crises which follow. There are many good books which cover human growth and behaviour in depth and we give references to one of these at the end of the chapter. We would re-emphasise the importance of socialisation and the development of self-identity, since distortions in these areas may have importance in the genesis, development and handling of psychiatric disorders. We do not say that such distortions are the sole cause of the development of psychiatric illness. A framework of possible causative factors has been developed by Cobb (1948) who gives the following aetiological classification:

(1) The role of inheritance in the development of illness, which can be subdivided into the genetics of the illness itself and the inherited predisposition towards illness.

(2) The effect of chemical agents or their lack. 'By definition this would have to be ruled out if the chemical agent led to visible lesions, or if emotional stress was the immediate cause of the chemical change.'

(3) Structural alterations of the central nervous system.

(4) The effect of stresses within the personality. It is this last cause that we will concentrate on, since it is this one alone that can be tackled at all by the average man or woman in the course of day to day living.

Valentine (1955) summed up succinctly, in the following analogy, the difficulties of ascribing causation of psychiatric disorder to a single source or cause: 'Suppose we are studying an apple's fall from a tree; gravitational attraction, of course, is the single "cause." But gravity is operating all the time; why didn't the apple fall before? Because the stalk only gradually becomes brittle enough to permit it to fall. But here is another apple, with an equally brittle stem; why didn't it fall? Because it was a little lighter; or wasn't exposed to the breeze as the other one was.' He goes on to discuss the ease with which an experiment could be designed to ascertain which cause was effective in the case of the apple, but pointed out the difficulty of designing an experiment to show why people develop psychiatric disorders; 'Because we have only a rough idea of what the variables are, and only a rough idea of how to measure them. If we study the person, we have difficulty in knowing how much of his history has contributed towards the disease; if we study the disease, we have corresponding difficulty in knowing how much it may have been modified by the personality in which it arose; there is no easy cross reference method to return a quick answer.'

However interesting and important the search for causes may be, *this book is concerned only to make the task of identifying the presence of a psychiatric disorder easier for the people who usually come into contact with it at an early stage*. Therefore, our approach is necessarily a descriptive rather than a causal one. Those interested in learning more about causation will find the other books in this series most useful.

references

Jahoda, M. *Current Concepts of Positive Mental Health*. Basic Books Inc. New York, 1958.

Langeveld, M. J. University of Utrecht. *Life as an Adult in the Perspective*. Paper presented to the International Round Table of Educational and Vocational Guidance. The Hague, 1970.

Tyler, L. *The Social Implications of Counselling*. Paper presented to I.R.T.E.V.G. The Hague, 1970.

Sarbin, T. R. *Studies in Behaviour Pathology*. Holt, Rinehart and Winston Inc. New York, 1967.

Report of the Committee on Maladjusted Children (Underwood Committee). Ministry of Education. H.M.S.O. London, 1955.

Cobb, S. *Foundations of Neuropsychiatry*. Williams and Wilkins. Baltimore, 1948.

Valentine, M. *Introduction to Psychiatry*. E. and S. Livingstone Ltd. Edinburgh, 1955.

recommended reading

Rayner, E. *Human Development*. George Allen and Unwin. London, 1971.

3 The neuroses

In this chapter we propose to deal with a group of psychiatric illnesses commonly described as the neuroses (sometimes referred to as the psychoneuroses). According to Henderson and Gillespie (1962), the 'term neurosis has, from the standpoint of classification, two connotations. In the first and historical connotation, its meaning is purely descriptive. It is a term referring to conditions characterised by certain mental and physical symptoms and signs.' They go on to say that the other connotation, from a medical standpoint, is more fundamental. 'This is to the effect that the existence of a neurotic reaction is an indication of mental conflict.' This latter aspect will be covered more fully from the medical angle by our colleague Dr Betts in a companion volume, entitled *The Minor Psychiatric Disorders*.

Since it is our intention to help the reader to recognise the presence of psychiatric illness, we shall, as we have already said, necessarily present more *descriptive* material rather than placing the main emphasis on the medical signs and symptoms. Nevertheless, because neurotic reactions are in the main caused by faulty responses to the stress of everyday living, and may arise from inner tensions that come about from unsatisfactory relationships with other people, we would find it difficult to split these two aspects in our presentation.

Although there is no absolute consensus of opinion about the classification of the neuroses, the following is accepted by most people:

Depression (Mild).
Anxiety States.
Hysteria.
Obsessional States.
Phobic States.

The foregoing classification will be expanded upon in the text, but it is worth mentioning that there are features that are common to them all. In the neuroses, there are no established physical causes, although they all have in common some form of disturbance of bodily function, which is not the result of physical disease, but which is due to, or associated with, disturbances of the psyche, although the patient may be unaware of the connection. Alternatively, they can take the form of many different kinds of 'unreasonable' fears, or of disturbed mental states, manifesting themselves in troublesome and obtrusive thoughts and disturbances of memory. *The outstanding feature of all these signs and symptoms is the fact that the sufferer is usually aware of their abnormality and their meaning; this compounds his feeling of discomfort.*

mild depression

Over the years, there has been much disagreement over the kind of depression we are about to describe. Some authorities divide this syndrome into two major categories – *reactive*, a response to some known stress, and *endogenous*, an as-yet-unexplained constitutional reaction. We do not propose to enter into this argument, but since the presenting symptoms in both of these conditions are much the same, our intention is to enable the reader to recognise them and perhaps to encourage him to leave the more detailed interpretations to the professionals. It would be impossible to describe cases that illustrate all the facets of presentation of depressive symptoms, but we hope that many of its features will be implicit in the case material that follows.

case 1 Mrs Jones

This lady presented herself at a social work agency. The reason she gave for calling was that she required help to find some form of voluntary or paid occupation. During her interview, Mrs Jones told the social worker something about her past life and the reasons why she had come. She was 52 years old and had been widowed some six months earlier when her husband died suddenly from a heart attack. Although she had a daughter, she had lived alone since this daughter married only three weeks before, although the daughter lived near at hand. She also had a brother living in the same area, who was married with two children.

Mrs Jones left school when she was 16 and worked as a saleswoman at a city store from then until she married, at the age of 27. Some time after she was married, she had some form of 'nervous breakdown' which she said had been due to the strain of caring for her bed-ridden mother-in-law and her new baby, but little is known in any detail about this episode in her life. She had always been very closely attached to her daughter and while her husband was alive she leant very heavily on him. In a subsequent visit to Mrs Jones's home, the social worker was impressed by both the tidiness of the house and her person. At this visit, she talked to the social worker about being lonely and as she spoke, she continually wrung her hands and her voice was rather dull, flat and monotonous. As she told the social worker about her husband's death, the tears began to fall and she was obviously distressed. She later said that his loss had left a great void in her life and that, although she had friends, she did not like to visit them because they were all married and their husbands were with them. She went on to say that, so empty was her life, she felt she really had nothing to live for, and that these feelings had not been helped by her daughter's recent marriage. She began at that point to introduce less positive feelings about her daughter by indicating that she felt she had been deserted.

Mrs Jones was concerned about her lack of confidence and ability to keep up with her daily chores, and she reckoned that worrying about this was interfering with her sleep. Even when she did sleep, she woke up in the morning feeling listless and felt that because of this she couldn't be bothered with cooking or even eating. She also blamed her lack of eating on the fact that she had become constipated recently.

Mrs Jones felt that being alone in her home had increased her feelings of loneliness and although she had TV, was fond of reading and particularly enjoyed doing crossword puzzles, she found that there had been changes in these interests. She found, for instance, that she could not watch TV plays through to the end and that if they were slightly sad, she would cry and then worry about this. The same thing happened with her reading. 'What on earth is happening to me?' she said. Particularly upsetting for her was the fact that the 'small jobs about the house' that her husband used to do, like mending fuses and doing small repairs were beyond her. But they also reminded her of his absence.

The visit paid by the social worker was near to Christmas time, and Mrs Jones began to reminisce about Christmases with the family. She went on to wonder if anything could have been done to diagnose her husband's illness at an earlier stage. Had this been done, she felt he might have still been with her.

The case of Mrs Jones is quite typical of what might be noticeable to friends, neighbours or relatives in contact with a depressed person and clearly highlights areas where not only general support would be useful, but also where specialist help appears to be called for. Before discussing this case at length, we will present another example of depression, where the symptoms were manifested in a way similar to those of Mrs Jones's, but also presented with disturbing effect in a work situation. We are deliberately presenting this second case because, too often, sickness is overlooked amongst friends and relatives, whereas in a work situation, pieces of behaviour tend to be treated in isolation and little allowance is made for the possibility that an underlying illness is causing deterioration in performance, so bringing criticism instead of sympathy. In fact, in the case which follows, it will be seen that not only was there no sympathy, but the person's illness was used as an excuse actually to criticise him.

case 2 Mr Sheldon

This case is presented as seen from the angle of his workmates.

Mr Sheldon, a man in his mid-fifties, had worked for the same firm since leaving school at the age of 14. A particularly conscientious man, who had applied himself well and by diligent, careful, hard work, had progressed to chief cashier, slowly and steadily, from his original post of office boy. He had worked quietly and unobtrusively and as a result had not made many close friends, at least in his work situation. He was therefore seen by some of his colleagues as a little aloof. Nevertheless, he was a very acceptable colleague, because he never appeared to interfere with other people and allowed them — indeed expected them — to get on with their work with the same diligence as he did his own.

At the time he joined the firm at 14, he was one of two office boys appointed. Whereas Mr Sheldon had come from a good 'middle class' home and went to a reasonably good school, his new colleague had come from rather poorer circumstances and had attended a school which was not noted for its high academic product. Their two careers took somewhat different paths within the same branch of the large organisation, his colleague concentrating on the despatch of goods to customers through various stages until he became a salesman.

The story really begins when the branch manager retired and a successor was being sought. Both Mr Sheldon and his colleague felt themselves to be very much in the running for the appointment and in the event it was given to Mr Sheldon's colleague. Almost immediately, Mr Sheldon presented himself to his colleagues as a very different person. From being an aloof, yet equable colleague, he became irritable and intolerant; where his work had been accurate and precise, the office now buzzed with complaints from staff at all levels about errors in their pay packets and in his work as it related to other people.

Changes in habits became quite marked — from being a very punctual and conscientious person he began to come in late and take an occasional day off without explanation. In effect, there was an attitude of 'couldn't care less' about work. Because he had joined the firm at the same time as the new manager, an affinity and understanding had grown up between them; this disintegrated. Not only did he show overt resentment, but presented this at a very personal level, by making public criticisms about his colleague, and making blunt statements that his intellect was so low that he could never be a competent manager. He became increasingly obstructive and negative. His old colleague had anticipated Mr Sheldon's disappointment and because of their long-standing comradeship made many allowances for this. These only appeared to feed Mr Sheldon's feelings of superiority over his new boss. Because of the close relationship, Mr Sheldon's colleague decided to refer the situation to the Managing Director of the firm because work in the local branch was suffering.

As a result, an interview was arranged between Mr Sheldon and the Managing Director of the Company, who was a very forceful man of decided views which frequently did not allow too much for the personal 'feelings' of his staff. Not surprisingly, the interview was rather one-sided. Mr Sheldon was neither invited nor given scope to discuss the situation as he perceived it. He was more or less told that his behaviour was so incomprehensible, that he must be 'sick'. Presumably because of his long service, he was told to take a month off and to have a holiday at the firm's expense. That was on full salary with hotel accommodation for himself and his wife, together with travelling expenses paid for by the firm. Although it may never have been said explicitly, the Managing Director's attitude was clearly one of – 'Have a good holiday and things will resolve themselves'.

On his return to his local branch, he told the manager that the Managing Director had obviously felt sorry for his 'mistaken' appointment and was trying to atone for this.

After his holiday, the situation did not improve at all; in fact it got worse, with more incompetence, more time off and increased irritability and intolerance of everybody. This culminated, as might be expected, in his being dismissed. From the firm's point of view he had been given a chance and had not taken it. Shortly afterwards he killed himself.

It was learned subsequently from his wife that, at home, he had presented almost all of the symptoms which were discussed in the previous case, but whereas he almost certainly received sympathy and support at home, he did not get either at work.

discussion

One of the main conclusions we wish to draw from both these case illustrations is that in mild depression, people tend to become preoccupied with areas of everyday life which, to some extent, we are all concerned about, and this preoccupation causes exaggeration of ordinary worries. Normally, people are concerned to some degree about their self-image and esteem, their relationships with other people, their competence, their health and their capacities for work and leisure. We have chosen these two cases to illustrate and emphasise that the symptoms of this illness are there to be seen, if one only pays attention to the fact that the sufferers have changed in some degree, and that their overt behaviour must be seen in its total context. Mrs Jones was, normally, an average, competent housewife, but being deprived of the support of her husband and daughter which had helped her to function normally, she became immobilised. We can see from the way she presented her symptoms that she did enlarge upon areas of normal concern – her housework became difficult, her concentration diminished, in that she was no longer able to read books through or to solve crosswords. We saw that her emotions became somewhat labile, in that she cried very easily and in relation to things that would normally have brought joyful memories, such as Christmas. The over-concern with bodily health can be seen by the fact that her appetite had gone and that as a result she was constipated – and her preoccupation was more with her constipation. It is very understandable that when one does not eat, bowel functions will diminish, but for her this rational explanation was impossible. We saw, too, that not only did her pattern of sleep alter, but its quality changed, since there were times when she found difficulty in sleeping and others when she did sleep but did not feel refreshed on wakening. We also noticed with Mrs Jones, that she felt so miserable that 'life was hardly worth living.' Indeed, in the second case, this feeling was so pronounced that it led to actual suicide.

Mr Sheldon produced some similar symptoms to Mrs Jones, but he also produced others that are common in depression, in that he became irritable, unpredictable and caused strained relationships with his colleagues, to such an extent that the normal smooth functioning of the firm became strained and at times even disorganised. In his case, we saw much more concern about his self-esteem and his self-image; there were also some indications that he felt that the world around him was treating him very shabbily. It may well be that he explained (to himself) that his depression was 'caused' by this. This is a most important aspect of relatively mild depression. When people feel as low in spirits as these two people obviously did, they have to find explanations for their feelings and, as we have indicated, from the areas of possible explanations that are readily to hand. These explanations are very necessary in order that the sufferer maintains his self-respect and even his sanity; without them, he may be forced to consider that his feelings are due to a malfunction of his mind.

It is very tempting to the person who comes in contact with depression to indulge in reassurances and to offer everyday solutions which would be appropriate for normal unhappiness situations, such as, 'You'll feel fine when you've had a holiday.' The difficulty is that often the person has a holiday and doesn't feel better – indeed he is liable to feel worse. Although, as we have said, people search for reasons to explain their low feelings, these reasons are frequently misplaced. Because depression can have an insidious beginning which affects normal performance, it frequently happens, as we saw in Mr Sheldon's case, that he could easily have blamed his depression on his loss of job, instead of the other way round.

We have mentioned how signs and symptoms may manifest themselves, but the case of Mr Sheldon stresses the essential need for the symptoms to be recognised for what they are, as expressions of an illness. In both cases, help of a very specialist nature was necessary. In Mrs Jones's case, she was fortunate in receiving skilled professional social-work help. This by itself was not in fact sufficient, but at least the professional social worker recognises the implications of symptomatic behaviour and knows how to arrange for more specialised psychiatric help, should it be necessary. Mr Sheldon was less lucky. His symptoms were treated in isolation – his behaviour was seen to change but his workmates failed to recognise the change in him, the *person*. There are now Social Service Departments in every town in the country where help and advice can be sought. This can be help for the sufferer, but also advice for the perceiver, if he is in doubt. It may be difficult for a friend or relative to make the initial overtures to the sufferer about the possibility of depression, but the general practitioner should, somehow or other, be brought in if it is felt that a depressive illness is present. Although in some cases the signs and symptoms may have been misread by a concerned person, it is better to be safe than sorry. As interested readers will find, in one of our companion volumes, depression is an illness which is usually amenable to treatment, but which is sometimes neglected at peril.

anxiety states

Anxiety neurosis is usually manifested by a morbid or pervasive fear or dread. It may occur as a symptom in conjunction with many of the other psychiatric syndromes, but here we are concerned to present and discuss it in those cases where it is the leading and predominant feature. Anxiety, in the illness sense, goes far beyond normal reactions to fear and worry. It tends to be more persistent and more disabling, but, fortunately, it is also a state that is reasonably amenable to treatment. The signs and symptoms usually consist of one or more of the following:

(a) Palpitations. (b) Irregularity of respiration. (c) Giddiness or fainting. (d) Feelings of suffocation. (e) Excessive sweating of the palms, or night sweats. (f) Dry mouth. (g) Loss of appetite. (h) Nausea and belching. Generally, the anxiety can be seen to be associated with some environmental situation, but, in some cases, the anxiety may be of a 'free-floating' nature – described by some people as a 'nameless dread' which attaches itself to a variety of non-specific incidents and events. A person, so suffering, generally describes himself or herself as being 'on edge', jumpy and irritable. The effect of anxiety is very tiring and enervating. The anxious person gets no real respite from sleep when he goes to bed; he is preoccupied by racing thoughts, unpleasant ideas and forebodings, so that getting off to sleep is difficult and, when he does drop off, he is often disturbed by nightmares.

case 3 Mr Wright

Mr Wright, a man of 35, was referred to hospital because of a 'dizzy turn' which he had experienced during his work as a labourer. He had had similar attacks in the past but, with each one, the associated feelings of panic became more acute. He felt that his wife and two children were being rather irritating and demanding of his time and energies, which he felt were diminishing.

As the attacks developed, he began to sleep badly. He had difficulty in getting off to sleep because of worrisome thoughts that raced through his mind; frequently his dreams had a menacing content and more and more they were only resolved by his awakening in a cold sweat, accompanied by frequent headaches.

Shortly after the first episode, he was investigated in hospital as an in-patient. During his time there, he improved, and no evidence of any organic cause for his fainting spells could be found.

Following discharge from hospital and in addition to the symptoms already outlined, he began to complain of pressure in the front of his head and uncontrollable trembling and palpitations. He became more and more dependent upon his wife and would go nowhere without her, in case he had a panic attack while on his own. This meant of course that he had to give up work. His condition - not unnaturally - brought problems for his wife and particularly for his children, with whom he found great difficulty in relaxing. In addition, his absence from work, or perhaps, more appropriately, his fear of returning to work, cost him his job. The worries about his failure to support his family caused his anxiety to 'spiral'.

We mentioned previously a kind of anxiety that is known as 'free-floating.' In order to illustrate this, and at the same time to give the reader some idea as to how this particular type of anxiety may originate, we will present the next case by describing the incident that led to the patient's development of symptoms similar to those displayed by Mr Wright.

case 4 Sgt Rourke
Presented to his general practitioner complaining of irrational fears, palpitations and many other anxiety symptoms which he had experienced for a period of about five years. He said that these feelings were totally strange to his normal functioning and that until the War he would have described himself as a 'perfectly normal' person. He could offer no explanation for his changed behaviour and, since the general practitioner could find none, Sgt Rourke was referred for psychiatric investigation.

The psychiatrist was able to locate a war-time experience of a most traumatic nature and was convinced that his anxiety began at this particular point in time, In a near-emotionless and abstract manner, the sergeant described his being in command of a tank which had been struck by a shell, and which had caught fire, killing one of his team. The manner in which he presented this dramatic incident led the psychiatrist to believe that Sgt Rourke was either unwilling or unable to talk about it. He denied forcibly that this incident had had any effect on him. By the use of a drug, the psychiatrist was able to take him back in time and 'into the burning tank', at which point the sergeant was then invited to react in the way that would seem appropriate to him. The effect of this treatment was that Sgt Rourke screamed at the top of his voice, shouted for his mother, and wept bitterly and uncontrollably.

Following this treatment, the anxiety symptoms disappeared. In this case, it looked as though the patient at the time of the event had behaved as a soldier 'ought to behave' but not as he felt he wanted to. Presumably, this resulted in his denial that he had any feelings of fear.

case 5 Mrs Banks
Mrs Banks was a married woman in her mid-twenties. She had made arrangements to go to a local Bring and Buy Sale with a neighbour. When the neighbour called for her she found Mrs Banks in a very anxious, excitable state. Mrs Banks confessed to the neighbour that not only had she felt like this fairly frequently, but the attacks had on occasion

been so bad that she thought she would die. Her state so alarmed her friend that she persuaded Mrs Banks to allow her to send for the doctor.

During her interview with the latter, Mrs Banks described herself as having been subject to nervousness and feelings of anxiety all her life. She recalled that, in her school life, she had been so crippled by these fears that she was occasionally unable to read aloud in front of her school mates.

However, she went on to say that she had learned to live with this disability and had not felt it really troublesome until about nine months earlier, when she reacted very badly to having some dental treatment. This experience brought on 'shaky turns' and her general health suffered. She said that her final collapse before the present episode was precipitated by hearing that an old school friend had suddenly dropped dead. Mrs Banks went on to say that she had been told that the cause of her friend's collapse was 'nerves which affected the heart', and added that she, too, had feelings of impending doom. To make matters more complicated, the doctor also elicited the fact that her father had died very suddenly from a brain haemorrhage.

discussion

The cases we have illustrated show some of the forms that anxiety states can take. They have in common a severely disabling effect, whose nature, as we have shown, is readily conveyed to the listener. Unfortunately, such people are frequently avoided because of the anxieties they arouse in others. They are also frequently referred to as 'natural worriers' and are often told to 'pull themselves together.' Unfortunately, no one tells them which strings to pull. There is a curious anomaly here when such states are compared with physical disabilities. For example, no one would tell a person with a broken leg to pull himself together and go for a sharp walk. This may be because worrying and fear are usually accepted as normal phenomena and it is difficult to accept exaggerations of them as an illness, though it certainly may be. Although many of the signs and symptoms in our three examples are similar, it should be noted that *Mrs Banks's* case presents an added ingredient – namely, that of the adoption of symptoms similar to those presented by both her father and her friend (i.e., she felt she might die, and appeared to be relating this to the fact that both father and school friend had collapsed and died very suddenly). This particular case is sometimes known in psychiatric nomenclature as *anxiety hysteria*.

We have tried to show that these illnesses can be every bit as crippling as a broken leg. However, people who suffer from them are to some extent avoided because of the ease with which their fears are transmitted. It is the authors' opinion that this avoidance is also frequently brought about by the onlooker's uncertainty as to how he should respond. We would suggest that relatives and friends can do something, if only by listening and giving support. They can also do what they can to ensure that the patient is enabled to seek professional help. For, as we have indicated, a lot can be done for pathologically anxious individuals by the use of psychotherapy and by drugs. The latter not only help to reduce the severity of symptoms, they make psychotherapy more easy to accomplish, since they enable the patient to co-operate with less effort.

hysteria

Fish (1964) defines hysteria as 'the presence of mental or physical symptoms for the sake of some advantage, although the patient is not fully aware of the motive.' There is a similarity between hysteria and malingering. The main difference between the two is that in the latter the motivation is more or less conscious, the symptoms are usually of sudden onset and they bear some relation to situations which the malingerer is keen to avoid. It is not our intention to dwell on malingering, but we consider it important to make a few points about it so that the reader may be better able to distinguish between the two. Some of the main differences may be summarised as follows:

(i) The symptoms are usually over-acted and exaggerated.

(ii) They are inconsistent with any single mental disorder.

(iii) The symptoms are only present when the malingerer is being observed.

(iv) They tend to be made to order. When it is suggested

that some symptoms of the illness being feigned are absent, the malingerer will usually try to produce them.

(v) When feigning illnesses, many of the usual signs and symptoms associated with the real illness are missing.

As was indicated in Fish's definition, the gain from behaving in an hysterical fashion is, unlike malingering, usually less apparent both to the sufferer and to the observer. For this reason, it is usual to refer to this as *secondary gain*. This is in contrast to primary gain, which is achieved in the first place by the illness itself. Secondary gains appear later and can be seen, in a sense, as by-products. The symptoms expressed by the hysteric can be categorised as follows:

(i) *Symptoms associated with the senses* – For example, blindness and deafness.

(ii) *Motor symptoms*, such as paralysis, spasms or tremors.

(iii) *Mental symptoms*, such as loss of memory (sometimes associated with a fugue or wandering state); pseudo-dementia (Ganser state), in which the subject acts as he believes a madman should; stupor (this usually only occurs under very severe stress); hysterical phobias (the patient is frightened of a particular situation – here the fear is gainful); and anxiety and depressive states, where the patient reacts to unpleasant situations with symptoms of these illnesses. The symptoms solve the situation to some degree, but are continued largely because of the secondary gain they achieve.

There are at least three special varieties of hysterical reaction.

The *first* of these is known as *compensation neurosis* and occurs when there is a desire for monetary or other compensation.

The *second* special variety, which is known as *engagement neurosis*, occurs when firm plans for marriage have been made, but unconsciously, there is a desire to avoid the responsibilities of marriage or to cling to mother.

The *third* of these special varieties is known as *anorexia nervosa* which presents itself as a failure to eat, nearly always in adolescent young adult females. Apart from loss of appetite, the sufferer may make herself vomit or take extraordinary steps to avoid eating when attempts are made to force it.

This, not surprisingly, leads to a weight loss which, in many instances, can be very dramatic. In addition, periods frequently cease.

case 5A Miss Wilson
This probationer nurse, aged 19, was causing much concern amongst her colleagues because, despite her unusual verve and activity at work and leisure she never appeared to eat and was fast losing weight. In conversation with her colleagues, her room-mate volunteered that she was worried on another count. Apparently, Miss Wilson's periods had stopped and though the signs were to the contrary, she wondered if her friend was pregnant. The group dismissed this idea, because they were aware that Miss Wilson rarely went out with boys and on the odd occasion when she did, the relationship appeared to be very platonic.

Miss Wilson had a sister three years her senior who had recently graduated from university with a good honours degree. She rarely talked about this sister and when she did, it seemed always to be tinged with envy.

In appearance, Miss Wilson looked very much younger than her 19 years and appeared to behave in ways that provoked irritation among her fellow-nurses because of her very demanding attitude. Sometimes she gave the impression that she played one person off against the other, and no matter which ward she worked in, there was always a modicum of tension and disharmony around her.

Despite her colleagues' worry about her physical condition, Miss Wilson did not appear to share their concern and even became aggressive at what she regarded as their interference, when it was suggested that she might be ill. However, when her weight fell to about six stones from her usual nine, her ward sister insisted on a medical examination because she was worried about the possibility of Miss Wilson having some communicable disease such as tuberculosis. She was also worried about her continual vomiting. The consultant who examined her could find no physical cause for her emaciated state and she was therefore referred for psychiatric assessment.

The psychiatrist found that, as a child, Miss Wilson had been something of a 'trouble-maker' within her family, despite her apparently reserved relationships. As with her colleagues, she tended to play one off against the other. As her colleagues had found, the psychiatrist also learned that her life pattern had been marked by an attention-seeking quality. For example, she was always the one who wanted to perform at parties and who would act in a provocative manner whenever visitors were present in her home.

The psychiatrist discovered that Miss Wilson was particularly ignorant about sexual matters and, in spite of her apparent provocative manner, appeared to be afraid of relationships with boys. Indeed, sex for her created many fantasies. So much so that she even imagined that kissing caused babies to be born. At 13 she had been a rather naive, but plump, little girl, who was frequently the object of teasing about her 'fat' tummy.

None of her relationships had reached any depth and, as well as her fear of boys and her general immaturity, there was no mature female figure in her life. Even her mother, said to be a very neurotic person, appeared to be remote from her. Father, a kindly man who had fussed over her a lot as a little girl, had had less to do with her as time went on, but this was more her doing than his.

This is a classic presentation of anorexia nervosa, and we have deliberately presented it at some length. We have done this because it is important that such cases be recognised as quickly as is possible, because of their intractable nature. Patients like this must be treated in hospital because of the extreme difficulties experienced in their management and, indeed, because of the possible risk of death. The outlook for full recovery is not completely optimistic: about one third of them fail to recover fully.

Hysterical manifestations can also occur amongst large groups of people; we see this frequently at 'pop' concerts and festivals, when young girls scream and faint.

A concept which underlies hysterical reaction is that known as 'dissociation.' Very briefly, this arises when the sufferer has a conflict which produces anxiety, but the latter is overcome by some manifestation of physical or mental illness which submerges the real anxiety. Because of the processes involved, it is noticeable in hysterical people that the emotions which should accompany events, or memories of these events, are often inappropriate. For example, one can be told a story by an hysteric which ought to produce sadness and yet it is told with a bland smile on the face. This is frequently described as *'la belle indifference'* – sublime indifference.

The following case illustrated *hysterical amnesia*.

case 6 Mr Webb

This man in his mid-forties was found by a policeman wandering aimlessly in a city centre in the early hours of the morning. Because he was unable to give any information about himself, he was admitted to the local hospital and was said to be suffering from amnesia (loss of memory). He could not even remember his name, but from items in his possession, his identity was fairly easily established. It transpired that before being picked up by the police, he was last seen by some members of the staff of the small firm he owned leaving for the bank to collect their wages.

Subsequent investigation revealed that he had not gone to the bank. He had been told by the bank manager the previous week that his substantial overdraft would have to be cleared before any further monies would be made available. Mr Webb appeared to be totally unaware of these events, but recovered very quickly when they were brought to the surface during treatment.

A common *conversion* symptom which is produced by the hysteric takes the form of fits which are superficially similar to those produced in epilepsy.

case 7 Miss Hall

Miss Hall was a nineteen-year-old assistant in a Children's Home. Shortly after commencing work, she had what the Matron thought was an epileptic fit. The fit occurred during a meeting of staff when job allocations were being made. Included in her particular chores for.the week was the task of helping in the laundry. Miss Hall was seen to sway in her chair, then fall forward and sideways on to the carpet, giving every appearance of a fit. On recovery, she told the Matron that she had not previously divulged her 'epilepsy' lest she didn't get the job.

The Matron, knowing a little about that illness, thought

that the fit had occurred because of the excitement associated with a new job, and that since Miss Hall had told her that her fits were few and far between she would continue to employ her. As time went on, there were more such fits, but it became noticeable to the Matron that they always appeared to occur when some job had to be performed that Miss Hall disliked.

Now for a case of *Compensation Neruosis*:

case 8 Mr Boulter
Mr Boulter was a married man, aged 45. He had three children and worked as a labourer on a building site. During the course of his work, he met with an accident in which he slightly injured his back. He felt convinced that the accident had been due to carelessness on the part of his employers. He was treated at home by his G.P., but as the minor injury did not appear to respond to normal treatment methods, he was subsequently referred for more intensive investigation which included psychiatric assessment.

He told the psychiatrist during the interview that he had been advised by his union to sue his firm for compensation. He thought that the whole legal proceedings were taking too long and complained that both he and his family were suffering because of this. During the course of the next month under psychiatric treatment his back still did not improve, but shortly afterwards his legal case was heard and resolved in his favour. He recovered immediately.

discussion

We referred earlier to other forms that hysteria might take. The three cases quoted are among the most common forms, although there are variations on these themes which are equally common. These cases do demonstrate, however, the concept of *secondary gain*. In the first case, we saw the need to ward off the bank's demands and Mr Webb's inability to face the inevitable confrontation with his employees. In the second case, it was noticeable that the fits allowed Miss Hall to be excused from duties she found unpleasant. In the third, it was clearly necessary for Mr Boulter not to recover before the assessment of damages was made. The cases of Miss Hall and Mr Boulter are particularly interesting. In the former case, the Matron, having some small acquaintance with the main features of epilepsy proper, was able to distinguish between this and Miss Hall's fits. Basically, the differences between hysterical and actual epilepsy are as follows: whereas hysteria is more common in females, there is no such distinction for epilepsy. The true epileptic has sudden fits, often without any apparent cause, whereas the hysterical fit tends to be gradual and to follow on some emotional disturbance. In true epilepsy, the sufferer not infrequently injures himself in his sudden fall, whereas, as we saw in Miss Hall's case, she avoided the possibility of injury by falling sideways on to the carpet. It was also noticeable in Miss Hall's episodes that these always occurred in the presence of other people, whereas the epileptic frequently has seizures on his own. In epilepsy, the sufferer during a seizure frequently bites his tongue and loses control of bladder and/or bowels, but this does not occur with the hysteric. Another difference is concerned with the behaviour at the start of, and during, the fits. With the epileptic, there is frequently a cry at the onset, but the hysteric tends to cry and scream *throughout* the episode and movements are often more violent and purposive than in the true epileptic seizure. Finally, the true epileptic often not only sleeps after the seizure but afterwards experiences a kind of 'twilight state'; the hysteric, on the other hand, tends to come to quickly and completely and, not uncommonly, accidentally reveals knowledge of what was going on around her while she was 'unconscious.'

The interest in Mr Boulter's case was the fact that his injury cleared up very quickly in relation to the compensation decision. In his case he won, but even in cases which are lost, disabilities tend to clear up equally quickly after an irrevocable decision has been made. It is the anxiety connected with the decision-making itself that seems to be important.

Earlier in this chapter, we drew a distinction between malingering and hysteria. Unfortunately, because the one is often mistaken for the other, the hysteric who is truly ill is frequently classed as a 'lead swinger.' This undoubtedly must compound the stress situations which activate the hysterical reactions.

We hope it will become readily apparent that, as with the other states we have described, there is a need for expert help, not only to handle the hysteria, but perhaps in some cases to ensure, for example, that the true epileptic or organically damaged person is not mis-diagnosed. It would be extremely unfortunate if injuries or brain lesions were overlooked because the observer thought he knew all the answers. It is important, however, that where a diagnosis of hysteria has been firmly established, attempts should be made to ensure the avoidance of stressful situations, since these may only serve to exacerbate the condition and impede its resolution during the period the sufferer is undergoing treatment.

obsessional states

The main feature of this neurotic condition is the feeling of being compelled to think or to do certain things. This tends to dominate the rest of the personality since it has an all-pervasive quality. The sufferer is acutely aware that his compulsive thoughts and actions are not only unreasonable, but are so completely dominant that normal work and living patterns are destroyed.

We are all aware of the person who is described as 'obsessional.' This is a variation of normality and usually means a person who is neat and tidy, perhaps with an accompanying tendency to rigidity. He has to have a place for everything and must have everything in its place. Very often, this is seen in the activities of the houseproud housewife, or the over-conscientious civil servant or the pedantic academic. However, such obsessional traits by themselves may actually enhance performance and one can imagine the ruinous possibilities for the banker who does not have these traits. Without them, he might credit one customer's account with another customer's money. It has been suggested that when such an obsessional person becomes neurotic he may be more likely to develop an obsessional neurosis than a person normally less obsessional.

When the person with a true *obsessional neurosis*, as distinct from an *obsessional personality*, develops *obsessional thoughts* as his main symptoms, these are very commonly of a religious or scientific nature. Not infrequently, these thoughts alternate between the morally uplifting and the degrading. The illness can also take the form of *obsessional fears or phobias*, which can be classified under many headings; the commonest of these are *agoraphobia* (fear of open spaces), *claustrophobia* (fear of closed spaces) and *monophobia* (fear of being alone). Another very common fear is often misnamed *school phobia*. In this latter case, the fear is not usually of going to school, but rather of leaving home, especially of leaving mother. We will not include in our case examples any of this last group since they are very adequately dealt with in the book entitled *Unwillingly to School* by Kahn and Nursten (1971).

case 9 Mr Blythe

Mr Blythe was a bank manager in his early fifties. He reported to his general practitioner that he was having thoughts which were repetitive and uncontrollable. His thoughts were recognised by him to be totally irrational, but when they appeared he was quite unable to either stop them or to carry on with his normal activities.

These thoughts took the form of the words 'Christ is a homosexual'. Nothing that he could do would eradicate the pervasiveness of these thoughts, so that by the time he presented for treatment he was in a very distressed and depressed state. This presentation is frequently referred to as a *compulsive-obsessional state*.

When compulsions such as those presented by Mr Blythe are acted out they can be even more crippling, as is seen in the following case.

case 10 Mr Bowen

Mr Bowen, aged 22, was an accounts clerk who was admitted to hospital as a result of the crippling effects of compulsive obsessions concerned with his personal hygiene. He had developed a routine for washing and dressing himself, which involved taking his clothes off in a particular order and folding them up in like fashion. These processes were so involved that, in undressing, he would frequently forget which stage he was at. He would worry about this and then have to begin all over again so as not to break the sequence.

So bad was his condition, that he was often in the situation of being quite unable to leave the bathroom for hours on end.

discussion

The foregoing examples are self-evident in their disabling effects and it is unfortunate that very often they are cases that prove very resistant to treatment. However, it is important to draw the reader's attention to the fact that it is not uncommon for an obsessional state to develop as a symptom, during a phase of a depressive illness. But in such cases, as the depression remits, so do the obsessional symptoms. This is an important distinction, since it is vitally important when describing the onset of any mental illness to a psychiatrist or a social worker to ensure that events are described in their proper chronological order. It is also important, since depression is an illness which is more amenable to treatment than is the obsessional state, although new treatments are beginning to give more hope of relief.

case 11 Mrs Arbuthnot

Mrs Arbuthnot was aged 56. She was married with a grown-up family who lived away from home. She had developed fears of such magnitude that she was totally unable to leave the house even to go to the corner shop.

This fear of going out developed after the marriage and the subsequent departure from home of her youngest daughter. It resulted in Mrs Arbuthnot becoming completely dependent on people coming to visit her and on her husband having to do all the shopping for her. After a period of months she became aware that people were visiting her with less frequency and that her husband was showing signs of becoming tired of having to do the household shopping during his lunch hour. Indeed, it was because of this that he brought his wife's condition to the attention of the family doctor.

discussion

Although cases such as that of Mrs Arbuthnot are described as phobic states, they have at their roots anxiety which, unlike the 'free-floating' type mentioned earlier in the chapter, is tied to situations or events. The patient apparently becomes convinced that she will not be anxious if she can avoid the situation with which the tension has become associated. Mrs Arbuthnot's case is a very common example of anxiety which has become phobic and has caused her to submit to a type of 'house arrest.' It is not uncommon for such people to remain in this situation for many years on end unless they have treatment. Usually, the fear is not so much of going into the streets but of *walking* in them and so the Mrs Arbuthnots of this world can be persuaded to take outings in a private car. Nowadays, treatments of 'circumscribed' phobias of this kind have become very much more effective than previously.

references

Henderson and Gillespie's *Textbook of Psychiatry* (9th edition). Revised by Sir David Henderson and I. R. C. Batchelor. Oxford University Press. London, 1962.

Fish, F. *An Outline of Psychiatry.* John Wright and Sons Ltd. Bristol, 1964.

Kahn, J. H., and Nursten, J. P. *Unwillingly to School.* Pergamon Press. Oxford, 1971.

4 The functional psychoses

In the previous chapter we dealt with the neuroses (or psychoneuroses) which are generally considered to be the minor psychiatric disorders. In this chapter, we will deal with the more severe mental disorders in which 'no evidence of underlying organic brain dysfunction has been proved to exist . . . The two main categories here are the *affective disorders* and *schizophrenia*; apart from being grouped together to make a neat classification, these illnesses appear to be quite independent of each other.' (Munro and McCulloch, 1969).

affective disorders

We will deal first with the affective disorders. 'Affect' is more-or-less synonymous with 'mood' and so the affective disorders are those which show an abnormality of mood as the most prominent feature; such abnormality may consist of either excessive sadness or excessive cheerfulness. Where the excess is one of sadness, the illness is known as a depressive one, and where it is an excess of cheerfulness, this is known as mania. Extremes of mood are easily conveyed to those in contact with the patient and it is usually possible to empathise to a considerable extent with his state of mind.

In Chapter 3, we also presented cases of depression, but these, as we emphasised, were relatively less severe and often more directly related to environmental stresses than the group which we now present. In severe or psychotic depression, the illness is much more intense, it is less obviously related to environmental stresses, and it may be associated with severe guilt feelings, suicidal thoughts, slowing down of physical and mental functions, more intense anxiety and delusions of guilt, and with bodily disorders. At the other extreme of the mood spectrum, is the manic state, when the individual is highly elated and over-excited. Very often a patient will display an alternation of depressive and manic phases and we then talk about a manic-depressive illness. The pattern of occurrence varies greatly between individual sufferers and the commonest consists of recurring episodes of depression, sometimes preceded in their early stages by over-activity and excitability, which are not dissimilar from some of the features of mania.

We wish to make it very clear that, when we write about a person's mood changing from normal, either in the direction of depression or of elation, we are not saying that everybody's 'normal' is the same. It follows, therefore, that one must know what the given individual's normal state is, before one can decide to what extent there has been a change. A good example of this would be to mistake the volatile and excitable behaviour of a person from a Latin country for a manic state, by comparing it with the notional normal behaviour of an individual from the United Kingdom.

Of particular importance with the depressed person are the changes in social functioning which occur (as shown, for example, in the case of Mrs Jones in Chapter 3); in severe depression, these changes are more pronounced and they may develop a delusional quality not seen in the milder cases. As we have indicated, people who are severely depressed sometimes present so many physical symptoms that the depression is heavily disguised and is only discovered after many physical investigations. Indeed, sometimes the depression is disguised to such an extent that it is only realised that it has been present after an attempted, or a completed, suicide has taken place.

During the illness, the mood tends to sink until it reaches

its lowest level and then, because the illness is usually self-limiting, it will tend to return to normal again, although in a small number of cases a chronic state can develop. Few people appreciate the depths of despair that may be reached, the feelings of unreality and the agonies associated with this illness – for the sufferer, everything is black and there is no future he can see that holds anything but disaster. It is for this reason that suicide is a common occurrence. However, when a person is so deeply depressed that his actions and his thinking are extremely slowed down, then sometimes he is unable to put his suicidal thoughts into effect. Because treatments nowadays are so effective and the sufferer can begin to be restored to his normal mood so quickly, sometimes the elements of the depression do not all clear up at the same rate and it is in the middle of his treatment that he regains sufficient volition to put his suicidal thoughts into action. For this reason, it is particularly important that the patient being treated in hospital for depression is not encouraged by relatives and friends to take his discharge because he is starting to feel better. The psychiatrist's opinion should always be taken and his advice should be reinforced by the close relatives and others. Because of the importance of this we shall now present a case which highlights this aspect.

case 1 Mr Noble
This was a batchelor of 52 who was admitted in a very depressed state to a Welsh hospital, following a suicidal attempt. Normally, he was an active, cheerful business man, with a keen interest in a local football club of which he was a director. His suicidal attempt was very badly planned and equally badly executed. It was recognised when he was examined by the psychiatrist that he was suffering from a severe depressive illness.

His story, as elicited by the psychiatrist, was that the treasurer of the football club had absconded with some of the club's money and he, as a director, felt the total responsibility for this. He said that it was all his fault, that he had worried about it for some time and, although the money had been paid back, he felt that he had let the club and all the supporters down very badly. He thought that he should be punished for this. This event dwelt heavily in his mind and he sought relief from his anguish by drinking heavily, although he was not a man who had previously indulged in heavy drinking.

He said that, coinciding with this event, he had developed severe constipation and that he worried about this also, because he thought he might have cancer of the bowel. His sleep pattern had altered, in that he had great difficulty in getting off to sleep and when he woke he felt totally unrefreshed and miserable all day. The only time of the day when he felt a little better was in the late evening. He had some idea that sleep would bring respite, but it never did. Eventually, his brother persuaded him to see his general practitioner. He had been very reluctant to go before, because he reckoned that his terrible feelings were a judgment upon him. His doctor recognised that he was depressed, but obviously did not appreciate the extent of his illness. He gave him sleeping tablets for his insomnia, knowing that he was alone in the house and that there was no one to supervise his pill taking. Forgetting that his brother and sister-in-law were coming to see him, as he went to take his pills before retiring one evening, Mr Noble impulsively swallowed the lot. When they arrived, he was drowsy and rapidly becoming unconscious and had to be quickly admitted to hospital.

On physical recovery he was transferred to a psychiatric hospital where he received treatment for his depression. He felt extremely well after a few treatments and was encouraged by his brother to take his discharge, but the following evening he went out alone for a walk, threw himself under a train and was killed.

case 2 Mrs Rogers

Mrs Rogers, aged 55, had lost her husband eighteen months previously. She had had a previous bout of depression three months after her husband's death, but this had lasted for only about a week and she had apparently made a good recovery from it; indeed, it was generally felt by her friends to be understandable unhappiness rather than depression. In her family background there was a history of depression and this appeared to have some bearing on her case. Her childhood had been normal and healthy and although she was shy, quiet and reserved, she was not described as having been unduly nervous. Her school life was uneventful, although she was not inclined to make friends easily. On leaving school she took secretarial training and became a competent and conscientious secretary. She remained in this post until she married at the age of 23. There were no children of the marriage. She had never had time to have children because she had been so busy with the house and looking after her husband. She was described as a house-proud person, who was neat and tidy about everything she did.

However, at the time of her admission to hospital, she presented a very different picture. She was dull and felt helpless and hopeless. She complained that her housework had got on top of her and that her concentration was so bad that she forgot things and couldn't relax. She spent much of her time pacing the floor and wringing her hands. She could not watch a television programme through to the end and couldn't read even a page of a book. She was full of remorse and guilt about her husband's death. She was convinced that had she nursed him properly and generally looked after him better he would not have died. She said she had been sleeping badly and just seemed to have been blundering through life, making one mistake after another and letting everybody down. She realised she was ill and took herself to her G.P. and thence to a psychiatrist. She easily accepted admission to hospital as an informal patient.

case 3 Mr Hill

Mr Hill, aged 45, was employed as a salesman in a men's outfitters. He first became depressed at the age of 37. He thought this had been due to his having to take over the managerial responsibility for a long period when the manager was ill. He had felt totally unsuited for the administrative burden of the job and was concerned that he might have been over-purchasing. He recovered without special treatment and remained well for the next 8 years, when the symptoms, unaccountably, returned.

He was normally a cheerful, active and optimistic man, who enjoyed his job because of his contact with people and the satisfaction that he got by meeting their needs. Nothing was too much trouble for him and he really was a very good salesman. He now found himself extremely tense and withdrawn. It was an effort even to speak to his customers and although his manager assured him that his work was still of a high order, he refused to believe this. He got no satisfaction or enjoyment from his work and even less from his usual leisure activities — to such an extent that he had given them all up. He said that he felt inferior to everyone.

There seemed to be no easily discernible cause in his environment which could be held responsible for his condition. However, he was worried enough to seek the help of his G.P. who prescribed some anti-depressant medication for him. This was not successful and he was admitted to hospital where he was given a course of electro-convulsive therapy (ECT). After a very few treatments, he made a rather unstable improvement which was characterised by a high state of well-being and over-confidence. So well did he feel, that he insisted on discontinuing all treatment. Unfortunately, after about two weeks this slightly manic state (hypomania) wore off and his wife encouraged him to return for further treatment, to which he agreed. After more ECT treatment he reached a level of improvement which was maintained for about six months, after which there was another relapse. Complete remission was achieved after a further series of treatments but during the next three years there were four similar episodes each of which was resolved by ECT.

As we have already indicated, mania is, as it were, the other side of the coin. In its mildest form (hypomania), people so suffering appear to display an abnormal energy and enthusiasm in work and social activities which are out of all proportion to the demands of the situation. As the illness develops, ideas begin to fall over each other and grand schemes for extending and expanding interests develop, although none of these is ever presented after due consideration, or in any detail. The individual readily becomes irritable and offensive if his schemes are inhibited in any way, by what he regards as the interference of the people around him. Everything is done at the double and there is rarely time even for sleep, because of the ceaseless activity of the mind. Expansive notions may lead to the laying out of more money than he possesses, drinking to excess, or becoming sexually promiscuous. Frequently a person with this disorder will write many long, rambling, almost incoherent letters, sometimes to eminent people, in which he puts forward his (to him) brilliant ideas. In spite of all this, his enthusiasm and high spirits often have a very infectious quality. This latter aspect is nicely demonstrated in the following case.

case 4 Mr Wagstaffe
Mr Wagstaffe, aged 23, was a car salesman who became ill during his first appointment as a salesman. He had been first engaged probably when he was in a mildly manic state. The enthusiasm which he manifested at this point was picked up by his potential employer and seen as a very valuable attribute. Indeed, the employer's confidence was not misplaced, for during his first three weeks he sold more second-hand cars than the firm had ever sold in a comparable period. He soon approached his employer and suggested massive alterations to the forecourt and showrooms and became quite aggressive when it was suggested that the success of the past few weeks might not last and that, in any case, it was easy to replace cars as quickly as they were sold, using the present adequate showroom accommodation.

Nothing daunted, Mr Wagstaffe told his employer that he did not recognise genius when he saw it and told him what to do with his job in no uncertain terms. He also told him that he would be very envious when he saw the vast complex of showrooms that he, personally, would own and run with the backing of an internationally famous motor manufacturer. He took action on his promises and wrote wild and extravagantly phrased letters almost daily to the managing directors of several leading motor manufacturers. He really believed that these would be well received and he described how the recipients looked and reacted when they received these letters, as though he were there to watch them. Quite unpredictably, he returned to his employer's premises one evening, smashed the showroom windows and damaged several of the cars. By this time, he had lost of a lot of weight — in fact he was exhausted and dehydrated because of the energies he had expended and the fact that there was never time to stop to eat. Eventually, he was admitted to hospital under an order for compulsory treatment.

discussion

In the four cases just described, we have tried to illustrate our point about the different presentations resembling the opposite sides of the same coin and we have indicated that occasionally the two extremes are seen in the one person at various stages of the illness, as with Mr Noble (case no. 1), who, though a clear-cut case of severe depressive illness, did display some over-activity as a preliminary to his main illness. Mrs Rogers (case no. 2), on the other hand, presented purely as a severe depression in relation to bereavement. In the case of Mr Hill (no. 3), we have seen that, during treatment, he moved from depression to mania, while Mr Wagstaffe (case no. 4), is a classic presentation of true mania, which began with acceptable, but overactive, behaviour which then appeared to get out of hand.

Mania in its extreme form is not seen all that frequently in this country, but milder forms are not too uncommon. In some people, the normal personality picture is one of great energy and almost excessive activity. It will be recalled that in Chapter 3 we pointed out some of the virtues of the obsessional person. The same may be true of the mildly manic individual who is, typically, the life and soul of the party and shows an abundance of ideas and an energy that communicates itself to those around him. However, it can become very wearing when the 'ideas man' never pursues his ideas to the end and never appears to take things seriously. Such people also have a quality of unpredictability and one never knows which way they are going to jump. When, as we saw in the case of Mr Wagstaffe, the condition develops into an illness, the elation affects the person's judgment and insight. He feels in better health than ever before. He thinks himself omnipotent and becomes convinced that his wildest ideas are in fact very practical. Because his memory is unimpaired, he is capable of giving rationalised arguments and explanations to support his proposed actions and this makes it very difficult for him to accept the need for voluntary treatment. It will be noted that, in Mr Wagstaffe's case, his behaviour had to become absolutely outrageous before he could be compulsorily brought into hospital for treatment. It must be pointed out that sometimes this manic behaviour, while being very disruptive, is insufficiently disturbed to allow compulsory admission to take place. By and large, our case presentations cover the main symptoms, but we would wish to point specifically to the hallucinations Mr Wagstaffe showed when he described 'seeing' the motor manufacturers reading his letters. Indeed, when he was questioned closely about this and asked 'How do you know they reacted like this?' he replied 'I saw them, didn't I?'.

Our three depressive patients all showed symptoms with which the reader will be familiar from his reading of Chapter 3. However, in each case the symptoms presented in this chapter are much more severe and we have seen that in the case of Mr Noble (case no. 1), there was also a delusional aspect to the disorders, in that he believed that he was suffering from cancer. In his case and in the other two cases of depression we have also shown that there was a marked degree of mental and physical slowing (or *retardation*, to give it its technical name). These three persons also displayed marked feelings of guilt, unworthiness and, in the case of Mr Hill (case no. 3), gross feelings of inferiority. Two of the cases, that of Mr Hill and that of Mr Noble (case no. 1) show that an assumption of immediate recovery may be not only misleading, but in the latter case was actually fatal. We have seen too, the importance of the part that next-of-kin can play in helping to ensure that patients remain in treatment until it is professionally regarded as complete.

All the cases in this chapter show rather more suddenness of onset than was the case with mild depression, although this is certainly not an invariable feature; some difficulty in thinking and in acting; marked self-accusatory delusions and reproach; and, in social terms, a crippling reduction in their competence in every sphere.

Although treatment for severe depression is not dissimilar to that offered for milder cases, it is more usual for the psychiatrist to want to conduct it on an in-patient basis; and if this is suggested, the relatives can help by encouraging its acceptance by the patient.

schizophrenia

'This term covers a group of severe mental illnesses which are not caused by any form of brain damage, but which show as a characteristic feature a very marked tendency to produce destruction and disintegration of the personality. In the majority of cases this disintegration is progressive and would result in permanent impairment of the mental state unless the patient received treatment.' (Munro and McCulloch, 1969).

The term schizophrenia tends to be misused in two main ways. It is often employed by lay people when they mean 'in two minds'; this undoubtedly having derived from the original meaning of the word, which was 'split mind.' It is also misused when describing the 'Jekyll and Hyde' type of character, with periods of complete sanity and periods of equally complete insanity. Neither of these usages really describes schizophrenia, for in this illness the personality shatters and disintegrates into a mass of poorly co-operating components, rather than into a neat division with two parts. In particular, there is an incongruity between thoughts and emotions.

main signs and symptoms

(1) *Disorders of thought*

There is a variety of ways in which thinking can be affected. There may be a difficulty in thinking in abstract terms and the schizophrenics' responses often appear strange because they concentrate on concrete things. For example, if asked to explain the meaning of the proverb 'People who live in glass houses should not throw stones' the schizophrenic will say something to the effect that 'people who live in glass houses and throw stones will likely break their windows.' In other words, the schizophrenic seems to concentrate more on the literal than on the proverbial meaning. Thinking also tends to be so over-inclusive that it is difficult to unravel and conversations on a particular subject are apt to include all sorts of irrelevant material.

Another sign of thought disorder is the common phenomenon

of *thought blocking*, in which the sick person's mind appears to go completely blank for a short time, to a degree which could not be equated with day-dreaming. It is of particular interest that this thought blocking, unlike day-dreaming, is particularly disturbing to the patient and is often associated in his mind with delusions that his thoughts are being stolen. Alternatively, when he is disturbed by alien thoughts, he is sometimes deluded into thinking that these thoughts have been forced into his mind.

Conversations with schizophrenics are frequently odd and stilted and are sprinkled with 'gobbledygook' or words created by the patient which are incomprehensible to the listener. These are known as *neologisms*.

(2) *Disorders of emotion*

Particularly at the beginning of the illness, a variety of emotional changes are possible. Common among these are anxiety, perplexity and sometimes mania. As the illness develops, there is a noticeable flattening of the emotions and the sufferer shows little reaction to events, although this flattening is sometimes interrupted by severe outbursts of rage, fear or hilarity. There is a marked incongruity of mood so that, for example, the schizophrenic not infrequently giggles when told something sad, almost as though his thinking and emotions had become completely detached from each other.

(3) *Disorders of volition*

Initiative is often deeply affected and is diminished to such an extent that the schizophrenic may just sit around apathetically, apparently oblivious to what is going on around him. In this state he frequently neglects his work, his family, and, indeed, all his responsibilities. Like the manic patient, he often talks a lot about what he intends to do, but rarely translates this into action. A noticeable feature sometimes shown is that of *negativism*, when the schizophrenic either refuses to do what he is asked to do, or does exactly the opposite.

(4) *Psychomotor symptoms*

Not infrequently, there appears to be a block between intention and the action necessary to carry out that intention. The patient may become completely motionless or even stuporose for long periods, interspersed at times with outbursts of violence. Although violent behaviour is very much the exception in schizophrenia, with some patients it pays to be aware that the possibility may exist.

(5) *Hallucinatory symptoms*

These are sensations which occur in the absence of external stimuli and are common in schizophrenia, when they are mostly of an auditory nature. For example, the patient may hear voices which tell him to do things. Occasionally, the voices say pleasant things, but more usually they are abusive and therefore frightening. Sometimes the schizophrenic thinks that his thoughts can be heard and that people therefore know what he is thinking. Auditory hallucinations can simply be noises like buzzing, but are often recognisable as environmental noises, voices and so on. Other hallucinations which occur, and which are usually unpleasant, involve taste, smell and tingling feelings which are frequently felt in the genital regions. These last may cause the person to think that he or she is being interfered with sexually. This can be very embarrassing for innocent bystanders who may be accused of assault.

Sometimes, the schizophrenic suffers from illusions rather than hallucinations, and in these cases the stimulus is real and he misinterprets it. Thus, a coat draped harmlessly over a chair may take on the shape and form of a frighteningly grotesque animal, out to do him harm.

(6) *Delusions*

These are over-valued beliefs which are false for other people, but to which the sufferer clings. They are very common in schizophrenia. Characteristically, there is often a primary delusion. This is something which suddenly arrives in the patient's mind like an inspiration. It is usually followed by secondary delusional beliefs, which appear to the individual to explain his puzzling new experiences. Not infrequently, these delusions are persecutory, grandiose, or of a religious nature.

Not every schizophrenic exhibits delusions and hallucinations and with treatment nowadays, many of these symptoms are prevented from appearing. Where they have been present, they often abate quickly as a result of drug therapy.

case 5 Mr Holmes

Mr Holmes, aged 24, was thought by his employer to be behaving oddly. His work as a clerk had been suffering for some months and ultimately he was dismissed because of the peculiar entries that he was making in the firm's ledgers and account books. Following this dismissal he had a series of jobs, none of which lasted for more than a few weeks. When he was not working, he was reluctant to get up and spent most of his time in his room, writing in a notebook which he secreted when he was not using it. Even when not in his room, he tended to do nothing in particular, although he did attempt to read light science-fiction books. When his mother, with whom he lived, tried to stimulate him into going out he said that he saw no reason to change his way of life.

He was extremely apathetic and totally lacking in interest of any kind. In general his manner was cheerful, but his attitude to his mother was one of complete indifference. He refused to go to see his doctor, but his mother wisely called the doctor in to see her, and while there, he managed to have a word with Mr Holmes. As a result of this consultation, Mr Holmes was referred for a psychiatric assessment.

During the examination, nothing abnormal was found in his early life circumstances, but at the age of 13, his mother noticed some changes in his behaviour. He had been given a camera as a Christmas present, but after using it once or twice, he said that he would not use it any more because it was giving him headaches. Following on from this, there were other examples of extremely odd behaviour, such as refusing to wear warm clothes in the winter, but insisting on wearing them in the summer time. He had frequent changes of mood which were not consistent with what was going on round about him. At school he never showed any interest whatever, though he caused his teachers no trouble. They regarded him as being a little odd but they had no reason for taking any specific action. He was a solitary boy and never showed any interest in sports or group activities. All his pursuits were of a solitary nature. He showed no interest in the opposite sex and when questioned about sex, he admitted very openly that he masturbated a lot. He made this kind of statement without showing any signs of embarrassment whatever.

Mr Holmes's father had left home when he was a toddler and during the years that followed his mother became increasingly over-protective and she encouraged him to stay at home with her, rather than urging him to extend himself in any way. A social worker who, with his permission, discussed the case with his last employer, was met with the comment – 'Sometimes when we had a conversation, I began to wonder which one of us was mad . . .'

This kind of schizophrenia is frequently referred to in the psychiatric literature as *simple schizophrenia*.

case 6 Miss Hurley

Miss Hurley, aged 23 was admitted to a mental hospital at the request of a social worker, who had been contacted by her mother. At the time of her admission, she was very disturbed, restless and extremely distractable. She had auditory hallucinations and during initial examination was obviously answering the voices she was hearing. She also had outbursts of totally inappropriate emotions (laughing or crying for no apparent reason).

During her conversation with the psychiatrist, she frequently punctuated it with facial grimaces and irrelevant remarks. At times she claimed that she had gone blind and also that she could not hear. The psychiatrist had great difficulty in making contact with her at any reasonable level, because she seemed to be responding completely to her hallucinations.

Miss Hurley was an honours graduate in physics and had been employed in laboratory work during the two years since her graduation. She came from a highly intelligent and successful family where academic success was highly regarded and both her parents saw a very bright future for her. An only child, she had been encouraged all her school life to try to match up to her parents' expectations, but until three months before her admission to hospital there had been no evidence that anything was wrong. Her illness was of very sudden onset and the delay in getting specialist attention was in some measure due to the fact that her parents had recognised that she was mentally sick but were reluctant to believe it, hoping that the symptoms would disappear as suddenly as they had arisen. Treatment was prolonged and of the many methods tried none was particularly successful. Although there were times when she became more normal, relapses soon followed.

This kind of schizophrenia tends to have a sudden onset and very florid symptoms. It is usually referred to as *hebephrenic schizophrenia*.

case 7 Mrs Smithers
Mrs Smithers, aged 28 was a housewife with one child of 4. She was admitted to hospital on a compulsory order.

Normally, Mrs Smithers was a fairly shy, quiet and reserved person and there were no peculiarities observed by her husband until some months before her hospital admission, when she began to withdraw into herself and spend more and more time in her room away from her husband and her child. During conversations with her husband and with others near to her, it was noticeable that she progressively produced more and more odd ideas about many things. She believed for example that brown eggs were that colour because, unlike white eggs, they were laid in the dark and that potatoes could see because they had eyes. However, when she presented odd thoughts of this nature, her family, particularly her husband, just thought she was becoming a little eccentric.

One Saturday, Mr Smithers went to his usual football match. When he left, his wife was her usual self, but when he returned some two hours later, he found her sitting rigidly in a chair and she seemed to be incapable of responding to his overtures of help. She had a glazed look in her eyes, and when he went to help her from the chair to put her to bed, he found that when he lifted her arm, it remained in a raised position, even when he let it go. During this time, she never spoke and when he persisted in trying to force her to go to bed, she resisted quite violently. So alarming was her behaviour, and so frightening, that Mr Smithers very quickly called in his G.P. who instituted arrangements for her compulsory admission to hospital. Even in hospital, she remained remote, was hallucinated and was liable to sudden changes from her immobile state into extremely impulsive, destructive behaviour. The psychiatrist told Mr. Smithers that she was suffering from *catatonic schizophrenia*.

The last case we will describe in this chapter is frequently classed by psychiatrists as a form of schizophrenia, but there are qualities about it which appear to make it an illness in its own right. Because of this it is often classified as a separate category of illness.

case 8 Mr Hodgson

Mr Hodgson, aged 54, married with 3 children, was a plumber by trade. For some time before his illness came to the notice of the medical profession, he had been unemployed. His mother had died when he was 15, and his father when the patient was in his late thirties. Although a plumber, he had had many different jobs in this line and had left all of them because of inter-personal difficulties and disputes. He said these disputes arose because his workmates recognised him to be a better workman than they were. Because of this, he felt that his workmates 'had it in for him'. Mr Hodgson had been previously married but left his wife, because he thought she was being unfaithful to him, although he had no proof of this. She subsequently divorced him for desertion and he remarried.

Mr Hodgson had always been described as a solitary, stubborn sort of man. He was moody, suspicious and could be aggressive. His home overlooked a football ground and he would frequently invite his workmates to watch football matches from his window, but inevitably these pleasant occasions led to accusations by Mr Hodgson that they were paying too much attention to his wife. Such accusations eventually led to his not even having casual friends. Another preoccupation that Mr. Hodgson developed was that he thought that when the groundsman at the football club looked in the direction of his house, he was trying to look through the windows at his wife, hoping to see her undressing.

On one occasion, just three weeks after his second marriage a stranger to him said 'Hello' to his wife when they passed in the street. This simple little incident led to a massive row which almost ended the marriage then and there. After he had lost his casual friends, Mr Hodgson became more and more suspicious of his wife and he would question her about who she had sat next to in the bus, etc. No matter what she said, he never believed her and inevitably a row would ensue. Following these rows, he would go to the local pub, buy himself a large whisky, and while drinking it, would muse over the row. By the time a second whisky had been drunk, he reasoned that the row was due to the fact that his wife couldn't like him. After a third whisky, he became convinced that she didn't like him because she liked someone else. Following several more whiskies, he would return home and give her a beating for her infidelity.

About six months before he was admitted to a psychiatric hospital, he said that he heard his deceased mother-in-law's voice whispering repeatedly – 'You've treated my daughter badly and I'll make you suffer'. This rather frightened him and he went to the doctor, who prescribed some tablets which he took very erratically, if at all, because he became convinced that the doctor was trying to poison him. During this six months he would either sit and stare into space or would pace the floor and smoke incessantly. He became more and more irritable and argumentative and at the point where he was forbidding his wife to go out of the house alone, the doctor was again called in and Mr Hodgson was admitted to hospital.

This case would be described as *paranoid schizophrenia* or a *paranoid state*.

discussion

In our earlier discussions about the cases we have presented we have attempted to draw together the features they have in common and those which were especially important because of their dissimilarity. However, since schizophrenia tends to be diagnosed in a less objective way than the illnesses previously discussed, we will not attempt here to link the cases in this section.

As can be seen from the examples quoted, the illness of schizophrenia often presents a quite characteristic picture, but when the features of these cases are analysed, item by item, it is noticeable that individually most of these features can be found in conditions other than schizophrenia (for example the apathy shown by Mr Holmes has a parallel in some depressive states, while the restlessness and distractibility of Miss Hurley could be found in some cases of anxiety neurosis). When asked to explain how they diagnose this illness, many psychiatrists will say that they use the criterion that there is a quality in the patient's behaviour which cannot be understood and there is no doubt that all the cases in this section would qualify for the diagnosis of schizophrenia, by this criterion of strangeness. An approach to diagnosis of this type may not appear to be very objective and our earlier comment about the informant who wondered whether he or the patient was mad, highlights one of the striking features of the illness. Since, as we have shown, one of the very striking features of schizophrenia is the patient's emotional aloofness, this often creates an atmosphere of oddness and apartness, which is difficult to pin-point though easy to sense. This sometimes causes the observer – even when he is a psychiatrist – to wonder if he is losing his grip. 'One can only learn this experience by dealing with schizophrenics, and, if the truth be told, one can only really learn about schizophrenia by coming in contact with cases which display the features of the illness,' (Munro and McCulloch, 1969).

We made reference earlier to a possible difference in the classification of paranoid schizophrenia and we would now like to point out the distinctions between this illness and the other three types described in this section. The word *paranoid*, broadly speaking, means that there is a disturbance in the relationship between the subject and the world, and delusions of both grandeur and of persecution are of this nature. We saw from the cases of Mr Holmes, Miss Hurley and Mrs Smithers that the content of their delusions were all different. Certain themes and concepts do recur, but in general, there is no fixed pattern of delusional material. However, in the case of paranoid schizophrenia, the content of the delusions usually tends to contain similar elements. These can be summarised as follows:

(1) Ideas of *self-reference*: this is when the patient believes that people are looking at him or talking about him, etc. These may range from only vague feelings to a firm delusion.

(2) *Persecutory delusions* occur when the subject believes that he is being persecuted by individuals or organisations.

(3) *Grandiose delusions*: this is when the patient believes that

he is some important person. These may present themselves as they did in the case of Mr Hodgson, who explained his workmates' antagonism towards him as being due to envy of his superior skill. These delusions can become so exaggerated that people sometimes believe that they are Napoleon or Jesus Christ.

However, it should be noted that, although the delusions described above are found in paranoid schizophrenia, they can also be found in other types of schizophrenic illness. But, whereas the delusional systems associated with the other schizophrenic illnesses tend on remission of the condition to be regarded, retrospectively, as flights of fancy caused by illness, there is a tendency for the paranoid schizophrenic who remits to remember them as though they had happened. He might say, for example, on reflection about his illness something like – 'Well of course, I would never have been ill, if it hadn't been for the police ganging up on me . . .'

reference

Munro, A., and McCulloch, W. *Psychiatry for Social Workers*. Pergamon. Oxford, 1969.

5 Psychiatric conditions due to old age or organic cause

In this chapter we shall be considering mainly psychiatric conditions which occur in old age; however, some of the *dementias* (degenerative illnesses) occur before the age of seventy and present similar pictures. The former are usually classified as the 'senile illnesses' and the latter the 'pre-senile.' When an old person becomes mentally ill, it is often felt that this must indicate some irreversible deterioration and that therefore there is very little that can be done for the patient. It is by no means inevitable that an old person with a psychiatric disorder must continue to deteriorate till death. Some mental illnesses which occur in old age are associated with a remarkably good recovery rate.

the normal process of ageing

For most people changes in the mind and the body occur more or less in parallel. If they have normally enjoyed good health, then the winding-down process is usually sufficiently gradual to ensure that they remain generally alert and useful to society right to the end of their days. Because of the common misunderstandings about the deteriorating process, we would emphasise that deterioration of mind and body in an old person does not mean that they become mentally deranged, although it can be seen that they undergo some diminution in certain aspects of their intellectual capacity. For example, the old person tends to be less clear about things that have occurred a day, a week or a month ago, but recalls vividly, and with relish, events that occurred in the long distant past.

Normally, people reach an intellectual peak in the early or mid-twenties and afterwards undergo a very gradual decline in the abilities which are concerned with abstract thinking, problem solving and the capacity to memorise. The capacity for original thought has usually diminished fairly substantially by the time the late fifties and the sixties are reached. There are, however, notable exceptions to this and some outstanding old people (such as the late Lord Beveridge, General de Gaulle, Bertrand Russell and others) retain these abilities to an extremely advanced age. In these cases, the normal slow process of deterioration is balanced by their great experience of life, their maturity of judgment, and their high emotional drives.

As people age, they tend to become increasingly less flexible in their attitudes, and they compensate for this by having 'set' patterns for living and by avoiding new situations. This process has a value in that, by the gradual diminution of their circle of friends, they are in a way preparing themselves for their ultimate withdrawal from life itself. Because old people in any case tend to become less active and their lives are more circumscribed, the process just described usually works quite well, but obviously it makes them very vulnerable to any sudden changes which are thrust upon them. For example, the elderly gentleman who, because of circumstances has to leave his home to go to live with relatives, or to an eventide home, may be totally incapable of adapting to the necessary new routines and this may cause him to become a little childish, irritable or even confused.

By sticking to a closely-guarded routine, some old people tend to annoy those around them by their fussiness, but it must be remembered that sticking with their regular habits protects them for, as we have indicated, age brings deterioration of memories of recent events rather than of past ones. It is fortunate that most old folk are able to fend for themselves, since their slowness and dwelling on the past can be very annoying to the younger people around them. It is indeed lucky that this independence is so often the case, since fewer and fewer young people nowadays want to take on the care of an elderly relative.

general aspects of psychiatric illness in the elderly

As a result of a community survey carried out by Roth and Kay (1962) it was estimated that almost one third of old people living at home in Newcastle-upon-Tyne suffered from some degree of psychiatric illness and that about two thirds of this unwell group appeared to be suffering from various kinds of psychoneurotic illness (the neuroses). This was a surprising finding since, until this time, it had been generally believed that these conditions were rarely found after middle age. Most of the severe forms of psychiatric illness found among the aged are also to be found in the population at large, but the general pattern of psychoses (serious mental disorder) is different and appears to be influenced by the difference in the mortality rate between the sexes. Generally women live longer than men and the latter are more likely to suffer from strokes and other illnesses of this nature. It is largely for this reason that women live on, to become victims of the mental illness which is associated with extreme old age.

the effects of physical illness on the mental health of the aged

It has been noted that there is a close relationship between physical and mental illness in old people and indeed, mental illness is often the direct result of physical disease, especially if the latter is chronic and results, for example, in either serious deterioration in sight or hearing. Such disabilities have the effect of cutting people off from sources of information such as newspapers, television and radio, and also from stimulation by others.

case 1 Mrs Williams

Mrs Williams was aged 78 and had been a widow for some years. She lived alone and was fairly dependent upon her neighbours and friends to help her with her daily chores. She normally appeared to be perfectly content with her lot until she developed cataracts in both eyes. As her sight became increasingly impaired, she became rather irritable with her neighbours and did not tell any of them that she was going blind. The result of this was that she became increasingly isolated and in the opinion of her neighbours 'odd'. She stopped taking her daily papers and books from the library and was seen about less and less.

She lived in a flat – fortunately a modern one with thin adjoining walls. In a way this proved to be a blessing in disguise for her. One night she got up to go to the toilet and as she went along the hall corridor, she saw a mysterious shape. She screamed and her scream was heard by the next door neighbours who came running in to see what had happened. They found her in a state of collapse on the floor, swearing that there was a man crouching in the hall by the door.

The neighbours, who had not seen her for some weeks, were alarmed by her agitation, confusion and general state of emaciation. It being the early hours of the morning, they contacted her G.P. and he in turn sought the help of the duty officer of the local services department, who arranged for her immediate admission to hospital.

There are several interesting features about Mrs Williams's case. (Incidentally, the legal aspects about her admission will be dealt with in Chapter 10.) On admission to hospital, it was found that her diet had been highly unsatisfactory, and that she had been eating little other than bread and drinking nothing but tea. This had resulted in a dietary deficiency which caused much of her mental confusion and this had been compounded by her poor vision. Thus the mysterious shape she saw in the corridor was no more than her outdoor coat which had assumed grotesque proportions. She was kept in hospital for several weeks, during which time her diet was regulated, and her confusion abated. Because of the state of her cataracts, it was not possible to carry out the necessary surgical operation and so she was discharged back to her own home, but this time under the care of a local authority social worker who arranged for meals on wheels and regular visiting by a local group of young volunteers, active in the field of welfare for the elderly.

In due course, she became completely blind, but a cataract operation was performed and in time she was able to resume her old, albeit restricted, way of life.

Apart from the physical aspects which this case illustrates, there is no doubt that isolation is generally bad for the old person because of the possibility of accidents – particularly by gassing or fire. Sometimes, an old person like Mrs Williams is unaware of her inability to cope and this very frequently results in the non-use of heating appliances with resulting hypothermia (extremely low blood temperature which in itself can cause death). For all these reasons, it is vital that any sudden changes in the life style of an old person (for example, even just their absence from their usual haunts) should be treated seriously and official help sought before a more serious crisis occurs (such as in the case of Mrs Williams).

the effects of bereavement

Bereavement causes a number of areas of change in people. There is for example the associated grief or reaction to the loss itself and this can be seen in several distinct stages:

(1) *Emotional numbness*. This can last for a few hours or a few days and it is usually characterised by an inability to take in what has really happened, or to appreciate the permanence of it.

(2) *Yearning or protest*. This is characterised by pining, which is usually intermittent and occurs mainly when the bereaved person has some sharp reminder of the loss of his or her loved one. During this period, there is a tendency to re-think all the memories which preceded the loss and there are signs which are normally associated with anxiety states (see Chapter 3). There is intense preoccupation with the lost person and sometimes a strong sense of 'presence.' Sometimes, there are also symptoms of depression (see Chapters 3 and 4) and occasionally, it is believed that the dead person is seen or heard. Frequently the religious person becomes very antagonistic about his or her beliefs. There is often anger and guilt accompanying the depression, along with withdrawal from social contacts and a reluctance to leave the house.

(3) *Despair* and *Disorganisation*. The sense of aimlessness

becomes more marked and the depression mentioned under *Yearning* represents an acute awareness of the disorganisation which has occurred. For the bereaved, life seems to have lost all of its meaning and one hears statements like '. . . I just stopped living . . .' 'There will never again be such a person as . . . was' 'When she died, I died too . . .' 'I had to keep going. I couldn't let myself give way. I never shed a tear. I seemed frozen. No one could see the way I was suffering.'

This stage gradually subsides, unless a true clinical depressive illness develops, and it is replaced by:

(4) *Reorganisation.* This is when the appetite and other signs of physical well-being return with the resultant aura of health characterised by a re-awakening of interest and a new meaning to life.

We have described here the normal processes of bereavement which are experienced to a greater or lesser degree by most people, but before we relate this directly to old age, it is necessary to discuss briefly some of the abnormal effects of bereavement.

The major abnormalities are either those of delayed reactions or of distorted reactions. In the former, the situation is often caused by the bereaved person having to pay attention to important matters or having to maintain the morale of other people around him/her. The delay can be very variable lasting from a few days to a number of years. If very late, it is often triggered off by another death, at which time investigation frequently shows that the seemingly current grief is really of very long standing. Lindemann (1944) outlined nine typical distorted reactions, as follows:

(i) Overactivity without a sense of loss . . . a sense of well being and zest – expansive and adventurous.

(ii) The acquisition of the symptoms of the deceased's last illness.

(iii) A recognised medical illness of the psychosomatic variety . . . predominantly ulcerative colitis, rheumatoid arthritis and asthma.

(iv) Alteration in relationships with friends and relatives.

(v) Furious hostility against specific persons.

(vi) In trying to hide this hostility (v), the bereaved person frequently becomes 'wooden' and lacking in affect or emotion, superficially rather like the schizophrenic see Chapter 4). They just go through the motions of living.

(vii) Lasting loss of patterns of social interaction.

(viii) Acts that are detrimental to social and economic existence . . . giving away belongings, foolish dealings and stupid acts which cost friendships. These acts are generally of a self-punitive nature and frequently lead to:

(ix) Agitated depression. This is a dangerous potentially suicidal state and even if the sufferer is not conspicuously suicidal in talking about intent, the danger can be spotted from the apparently very strong desire for self-punishment in the ways previously indicated.

We hope that it will have become obvious from the above descriptions of normal and abnormal reactions to bereavement, that if they are difficult for young people to deal with in themselves, they are even more difficult for the elderly because, as we pointed out earlier, their patterns of living are more circumscribed and their ability to accept change is substantially diminished. The elderly survivor may find it well-nigh impossible to change long established habits and may pine away in his or her isolation because accustomed patterns of life (including eating habits) are no longer there to sustain and comfort.

Some distorted reactions can easily be spotted, but we also present a case which is less obvious in order to demonstrate the need to be on the alert for what is happening when an old person loses his or her partner:

case 2 Mrs Harris

Mrs Harris; aged 82, had been married for almost fifty-one years when her husband died very suddenly as a result of a stroke. She had four grown-up children, all married and living away from home. They were all very distressed at their father's death. Indeed, so distressed were they, that none of them was really able to take the initiative in helping their mother and it was left to her to arrange for the funeral etc.

Mrs Harris was regarded by all who knew her as being an

'absolute brick' and they rather marvelled at her composure in the way she supported the children, although one or two friends did remark at her apparent lack of grief.

After the funeral was over and her family had gone home, it was noticeable that she did not seem to want the attention of her many friends. However, they tended to ignore her requests to be left alone and to force themselves upon her. This appeared to result in Mrs Harris becoming openly hostile towards them and making accusations against a few of them, to the effect that they were glad about what had happened . . . because in some way they had it 'in for' her. After a short period of this hostile behaviour, she became very formal with the people who called and appeared to lack any zest for life. Not even her family could instil any life into her. After a few weeks she began to dispose of valuable possessions, despite protestations from the recipients — mainly her children. From being almost automatic in her responses she became very agitated and depressed (see Chapters 3 and 4) and it was assumed by those around her that this was merely a late reaction to her loss, which they thought she would get over. Unfortunately, when her son came to see her one evening and could get no reply to repeated knockings, the house was forcibly entered. His mother was found dead with her head in the gas oven.

In the case of Mrs Harris, the comment made by her friends that her depression was merely delayed grief was of course only a part-truth, because she had certainly shown no grief reactions immediately after her husband's death. The important thing for the reader to realise is that the absence of appropriate grief *is* the evidence of a delayed reaction and *not* the more depressive-seeming illness which can follow. When it becomes apparent to observers that a person is not showing a grief reaction there are some things that they might do to help. We give below the most important of these:

(1) It is advisable not to steer conversations directly on to the death itself, but at least to acknowledge openly that it has taken place and that it is understood how people *feel* in such a situation.

(2) It is helpful to suggest that talking about how one feels in situations like this can help.

(3) The lay person should not attempt to offer explanations about the bereaved person's feelings, since such an emotional experience cannot really be explained by another person.

(4) It is often advisable to direct the conversation on to the 'old days' since this allows for some appreciation of the bonds that *exist* and it also allows the bereaved person to begin to get things into proper perspective.

(5) It would be easy for someone to attempt to interpret the feelings of such people as Mrs Harris, by explaining that the absence of overt sorrow was due to the fact of her taking care of the family. This kind of interpretation is not helpful. It is more important to try to help the bereaved person to talk about *her* feelings.

(6) It is best to allow the bereaved person to move at her own pace during these encounters, since it can be too overwhelming to allow all the feelings of a life-time of marriage to pour out in an uncontrolled way.

(7) When it is felt that the feelings have been talked out, then it is time to begin gently to talk about the future – at least to indicate that there *is* a future.

psychosis in old age

Roth (1955), in a paper entitled 'The Natural History of Mental Disorder in Old Age' found that with few exceptions, a hospital population of elderly psychotic patients fell into five main categories:

(i) Affective Disorders (these have been largely dealt with in Chapter 3).

(ii) Senile Dementia.

(iii) Arteriosclerotic dementia (disturbance of the blood supply to the brain due to the hardening of the aerteries).

(iv) Acute confusional states (typified by the case of Mrs Williams).

(v) Late paraphrenia.

Earlier in this chapter we indicated that, besides *senile dementia*, there was also a similar condition which occurs earlier in life, known as *pre-senile dementia*. Because of the similarity in presenting symptoms we propose only to describe two cases of dementia in the older age-groups, one of the senile type and one largely due to arteriosclerosis.

case 3 Mrs Grainger

Mrs Grainger, aged 70, was married, with two unmarried daughters both living at home. She had always been a good housewife and mother and had a reasonably good health record.

Her family began to notice that she was becoming a little forgetful about everyday things and that her forgetfulness was causing her a lot of anxiety. For instance, she would go shopping and forget what it was she went to buy, or alternatively would leave her purchases or her change on the shop counter. This forgetfulness became progressively worse, until she reached a stage when, for example, she would peel the potatoes, put the peelings in the pot and throw away the potatoes. More and more frequently she would lost her way home from shopping by getting on the wrong bus and, to the consternation of her family, would arrive home hours late.

As time went on, her mental activities became slower and her memory more and more inadequate. There were severe outbursts of agitation, panic, and, unusually for her, of anger. Her social behaviour deteriorated, in that she failed to dress properly or to take care of her personal appearance. More and more she became childlike, especially as regards her eating habits. She would want her sweet before her soup if she felt like it and embarrassed the family by removing her dentures and putting them on the table, saying that her gums were sore. She became very unstable emotionally with laughter or foolish behaviour alternating with periods of crying and depression. After a period of just over a year, she reached a stage when the family could no longer keep her at home, especially as she had become incontinent and would totter around the house doing dangerous things like turning on the gas and forgetting to light it, or spilling boiling water when trying to make the tea.

She died some four months after admission to hospital.

case 4 Mr Watt

Mr Watt, aged 66 was a retired bank manager. He had always been a very competent, but rather fussy, obsessional individual, who showed many of the characteristics we outlined when dealing with obsessional states in Chapter 3. Mr Watt was married, with a daughter who had left home when in her late teens. He was not the easiest of men to get on with, because of his rigidity and, at times, his short temper. As a result he had a somewhat strained relationship with his wife and had few close friends.

He had suffered from high blood pressure for some years and at the age of 55 suffered from a mild, cerebral thrombosis which probably indicated a degree of arteriosclerosis. From being a man who prided himself on his good memory, after his stroke he found it necessary to carry a diary, otherwise he would forget even important appointments. He became even more rigid and very touchy. In addition, he became increasingly careless in his dress and his jacket was always be-spattered with food. Indeed, his inability to handle staff brought about his early retirement at the age of 57. When asked how he felt about this, he broke down into tears and it was learned from his wife that his emotions had become very labile about many things. Following his retirement, the relationships at home became very strained indeed, particularly since his wife did not recognise his forgetfulness as being any more than an exaggeration of his now general awkwardness. More and more frequently, he became overexcited or irritable, with periods of deep depression which lasted for some weeks.

He was given drugs for his depression and for his blood pressure and this brought a new forcefulness to his behaviour. He appreciated how much his illness was affecting his behaviour and how it restricted him in his relationships with other people. It was probably because of this insight that the periods of depression occurred. Coupled with this, his impatience frequently made him threaten to take his life when things were not going his way. He felt, between depressive bouts, that he should be gainfully employed, but never quite got around to doing anything about it.

His daughter, who had left home when in her teens, returned after a two year absence and announced that she was going to marry a man of a different religious faith. This produced an enormous family row which culminated in his daughter leaving home saying that she would never return and his wife threatening to go with her. Before his wife could leave, however, Mr Watt had a severe stroke which resulted in his death.

Both the above cases are examples of an irreversible dementing process and they have in common an impairment of recent memory, a slowing of intellectual function and a deterioration in social habits. In both cases, it is noticeable that there was insight into the fact that something was wrong and this caused agitation and depression, although this was more pronounced in the latter than in the former instance. It is also noticeable that both these persons died fairly soon after the onset of the deterioration. This is consistent with Roth's (1955) findings that, after two years of being hospitalised, 80% of the senile dementias and 70% of the arteriosclerotic dementias had died.

It is important to recognise that in illness of this type, the close relatives, if supported, can maintain their sick member at home until the later stages of the illness are reached. It is probably obvious, from our description of Mrs Grainger's case, that much of her anxiety could have been relieved had she been protected from the experiences which were highlighting the fact that there was something wrong with her.

For example, had members of the family done the shopping and the cooking, many of the incidents which were so distressful to her would have been forestalled.

While one cannot offer much hope of recovery in cases of this kind, it is possible to keep a family together by supporting the other members, but it takes skilled help in getting the relatives to realise that there is no improvement possible and to give them the kind of support that is so necessary. It will be appreciated that to watch a loved one slowly deteriorating is very stressful indeed. There is little comfort for the family in simply being told that by the time hospital treatment is necessary, their sick member will have no insight into what is happening to them – this, as we have indicated, takes great competence to handle.

The other main psychosis experienced by some old people is paraphrenia, or late paraphrenia. This illness includes a rather mixed group of patients, but a fairly large proportion of them appear to be suffering from schizophrenia of late onset. Where old people are concerned this usually assumes the paranoid form (see Chapter 4). It is much more common in the divorced and in the unmarried (especially unmarried women). The people who suffer from it frequently live to a great age and in some cases it is suggested that it is the patient's extreme longevity with its subsequent isolation from the contemporaries, who predecease them, that precipitates it. Not infrequently it appears that this illness has been brought on by a disability such as deafness, which aggravates loneliness. There are some cases, however, which appear to be associated with some chronic form of personality disorder – usually of the schizoid type (see Chapter 6).

case 5 Miss Slingsby
Miss Slingsby was aged 84. She lived by herself on a Council estate where there were many children. She was the only single woman in her block of flats. Since coming to the area some twenty-five years earlier, she had kept herself to herself and apparently had no close friends and only one surviving niece who had any contact with her. At the age of 70, she found that she was becoming increasingly hard of hearing and by the age of 75 was equipped with a deaf aid.

When she was 80, her niece died and she became totally isolated. From this time her sole contact was her G.P. who never failed to call in to see her whenever he was in the district. He became aware, after a time, that her usual complaints about the noisy children around her were assuming much greater proportions, but felt that this was only her way of providing conversation which would detain him for longer periods than he was used to spending. As a result, with her permission, he arranged for a social worker to call on her. The social worker was made very welcome, but soon, she too noticed that the complaints about the children's noise now included the fact that they were playing outside her windows all through the night. Miss Slingsby also complained about the persistent crying of the baby of the people upstairs and asked the social worker if she could do something about this. So earnest was her plea that the social worker called on the neighbours, only to learn that there were no children in the house at all and moreover none ever visited. When this was pointed out to Miss Slingsby, she became very irate and wondered if the social worker thought she was out of her mind. She asked the social worker not to call again, but did in fact receive her when she paid a further visit. As time went on, Miss Slingsby's complaints began to assume even greater proportions and she complained that not only were the children upstairs noisy, but, they were not allowing her to get to sleep because they were throwing stones at her windows and flashing lights through them.

Soon she began to telephone the police in the middle of the night, making similar accusations and eventually she was admitted to hospital on a compulsory order. This was necessary as she saw the whole thing as being real and no amount of reasoning would dissuade her from this.

The case of Miss Slingsby highlights most of the common symptoms of paraphrenia. We would especially point to the solitariness of her habitual way of life. Her illness was precipitated, as we have seen, by a combination of two events – her niece's death, and her own deafness. Indeed, she had also complained to the social worker that the children were causing strange noises to be transmitted through her hearing aid. Presumably this arose from the fact that as she became more deaf, the appliance became less effective. This secondary delusion must have added greatly to her generally bewildered state. People like Miss Slingsby are very difficult to help for, as we have seen, even a skilled social worker was relatively unable to achieve much before she finally broke down completely.

specific organic states

As we have indicated, a person who suffers from a chronic dementing illness presents many social problems and is unlikely to be able to carry out his normal social tasks. His behaviour may be very difficult and unpredictable at times and treatment may involve his family in much time and trouble. In addition to these dementing illnesses, there are other organic conditions which are common and which also produce social problems.

case 6 Mr Samson

Mr Samson, aged 35, was a married man with two young children. He had an extremely good work record with his local Corporation, first as a bus conductor and for the past five years as a driver. He had always been an easy-going, tolerant fellow and was an excellent husband and father, spending all his available spare time with his family. One day he was involved in an accident in which he sustained a serious head injury. He was unconscious for ten days. Altogether he was in hospital for six months, during which time there were periods of delirium and he subsequently could not remember the events leading up to, or following, his accident.

By the time he was discharged from hospital, he appeared to have recovered physically, but he was not the same person. From being a considerate father, he had become intolerant of any noises that the children made and spent as little time with them as he could. Indeed, he took to staying out during their waking time, returning only when they were in bed. This was usually late at night and he was usually intoxicated. He became not only irritable but physically abusive to his wife. Although his employers were happy to wait for his complete recovery to re-employ him, he gave up his job in a very abrupt manner. His mood became quite unpredictable and he would cry at the least provocation. There were also complaints of headaches, nausea and giddy turns. These were associated with complete irresponsibility and, when he had physically abused his wife, complete lack of remorse. These personality changes were present to such a degree that they were very similar to the characteristics of the personality disorder labelled psychopathic (see Chapter 6).

The symptoms of change shown by Mr Samson, not uncommonly occur after severe brain damage but are not by any means inevitable. The amount of personality change which takes place is related to the extent and site of the brain injury. Epilepsy, with or without personality changes, can result from similar injuries. In Chapter 3, we discussed the symptoms of epilepsy because it seemed to be appropriate to help the reader to distinguish between this and hysteria (see the case of

Miss Hall) – but it is, truly, an organic illness. We would stress that the great majority of epileptics are in most cases perfectly normal mentally, between fits. This is in contrast with the permanently changed state of Mr Samson. However, like Mr Samson, whose new irresponsibility and irrational behaviour should really prohibit him from driving any form of motor vehicle, the epileptic, because of the sudden onsets of fits, is likewise prohibited. In addition, the epileptic whose fits are not totally under control, is well advised to restrict his occupation to jobs which avoid heights or avoid work with machinery. Unlike Mr Samson's condition, treatment for epilepsy can, in most cases, control the frequency of seizures and increasingly the lives of epileptic patients can be more or less completely productive and normal.

Many cases of head injury are not quite so dramatic in their effects as those seen in the case of Mr Samson. But frequently, there are minor personality changes such as increased irritability and moodiness, although these changes are often transient and do not involve the whole personality.

In addition to physical brain damage caused by accident, the brain can also be damaged by some viruses or by other infectious illnesses. Fortunately, these cases are becoming increasingly rare and we do not propose to do more than mention some of the illnesses involved. The most noticeable illness which causes brain damage is syphilis, but with early treatment this is certainly a rarity nowadays. Still fairly common, however, is the organic brain damage caused by brain tumours, meningitis or encephalitis. So far as the last of these is concerned, this will be covered a little more fully in Chapter 9.

In all cases of psychiatric conditions due to old age or to organic causes, the aim should always be to support the families of such patients, for once the family has accepted the medical situation, social help can be provided to enable the patient to remain at home for as long as possible. Where the patient has a recoverable disorder, which nevertheless causes persistent symptoms or some degree of personality abnormality, the family may need practical help, emotional support and assistance to enable them to reduce their expectations of the patient.

references

Roth, M., and Kay, D. W. K. (1962). 'Social, Medical and Personal Factors associated with Vulnerability to Psychiatric Breakdown in Old Age.' *Geront. Clin.* 4, 147–160.

Lindemann, E. (1944). 'Symptomatology and Management of Acute Grief.' *American Journal of Psychiatry.* Vol. 101, September.

Roth, M. (1955). 'The Natural History of Mental Disorder in Old Age.' *J. Ment. Sci.* 101, 281.

6 Abnormalities of personality and psycho-sexual disorders

the personality disorders
This is a group of disorders in which the basic personality is noticeably abnormal. There is some disagreement as to whether disorders of the personality can be regarded as mental illnesses as such, since in many instances they are so described only when they appear at the extreme end of a range of behaviour from 'relatively normal' at one end to 'extremely deviant' at the other. It is difficult, also, to be precise about what is normal (see Chapter 2), since such a decision is based largely on value judgements which vary according to historical time and social setting. There is a tendency for us to judge normality by people who differ *markedly* from the group to which we ourselves belong. For example, an exceedingly intelligent or an exceedingly dull person is often considered to be abnormal by average standards, although there are many people at both ends of this scale in the community. 'The average man is a statistical myth, and in so far as we deviate psychologically in one way or another from the notional mean, we all suffer from personality abnormalities. In the great majority of instances, the deviation, whatever it is, is perfectly acceptable and neither the person nor society is any worse off for its existence.' (Munro and McCulloch, 1969.)

We would emphasise that in this chapter we are dealing

with personalities which are in the main very different from what can be accepted as normal by the majority of people. We would also emphasise that, though the cases we shall describe concern only disorders of personality, it must be remembered that, besides having an abnormal personality, it is possible also to suffer from any of the illnesses we have already described.

A serious abnormality of personality often manifests itself at an early age and there is frequently a history of difficult behaviour during childhood. Such difficulties may present as excessive quietness, restlessness, aggressiveness, or even delinquency, but tend to become much more obvious in early adolescence which, as we have indicated, is an explosive phase in normal development.

Generally, persons showing personality abnormalities of any degree also show a fairly marked degree of inadequate social behaviour, which is not necessarily related to intelligence. This inadequacy often takes the form of poor interpersonal relationships, poor work record, lack of consistency of drive and brushes with authority, including the law. But it does not necessarily follow that the *personality disordered* person must necessarily be a social failure. Indeed, many very successful business tycoons and actors display many of the facets we describe.

There is some dispute as to the origins of personality disorder, but in the more serious cases we shall present, there is often a history of disturbed early upbringing and a lack of consistent parental care; it would appear that these aspects do play a very important part though not necessarily exclusively. As we pointed out in the last chapter, some personality disorders can be the result of brain damage caused by injury or illness. There are some schools of thought which are quite definite in their view that genetic inheritance can also play a part, but to date the products of research in this field are not at all conclusive. Some people seem never able to 'grow up,' or to be able to meet the normal viscissitudes of life – they are often referred to as being either *immature* or *inadequate*. Unfortunately, people are so described for derogatory reasons and although the terms can be useful clinically, they should not be over-used in general classifications. The use of these words is mainly descriptive and we will not therefore present them as special categories.

case 1 Miss Webster

Miss Webster, aged 21 was employed as a secretary in a large industrial concern. She was a pretty girl, with many friends of both sexes and her company was enjoyed because she laughed so easily at the 'little things'. One side of her personality which was noticeable to her colleagues was, that although she worked fairly competently, she continually sought reassurance about her work and was very easily upset if she thought she had not produced a perfect piece of work. She had an unfortunate trait, in that when asking for advice or help she would always remark 'how clever' the other person was and how she envied this. She had many little mannerisms of a nervous nature besides her tendency to giggle, such as blushing easily and profusely and by the ease with which she became embarrassed.

She used to worry a lot about little things but this did not upset her unduly. At work she always liked her 'in-tray' to be empty, and though, when giving her new work, her boss frequently told her that there was no urgency, it became noticeable that when she had a lot of work on hand, its quality deteriorated considerably and frequently tears ensued.

Normally, she took her holidays during the firm's slack period, but one year the idea of a holiday abroad with some friends at Easter time was so attractive that for the first time she broke with tradition. On her return from holiday, which was at the end of the firm's financial year, the work that had accumulated for her was massive and she was totally incapable of making a start on it.

In addition to her normal worrying, she became depressed (see Chapter 3), and was encouraged to consult the firm's doctor. He arranged for her to be seen by a psychiatrist who diagnosed a mild depressive illness in a basically *anxious personality*.

anxious personality

It is important to note that with treatment Miss Webster's depression was fairly quickly relieved but the anxiety, which was part of her normal self, remained. However, she was restored to the state in which she could function and her colleagues had now become aware of her vulnerability and were more supportive. Her boss, for example, tended to keep his non-urgent work on his own desk and would only give it to her as and when her 'in-tray' was seen to be almost empty.

Here, although we have a picture of a rather nervous 'worrier,' we also have a person who was generally fairly happy with her life and whose personality was in many ways attractive. Although we have seen that overwork (in her opinion) tended to cripple her, she was nevertheless very conscientious and a good staff member. The particular points to notice are Miss Webster's progression from an *anxious personality* to an anxiety state and, subsequently, to a depressive illness. People with a personality of this type can often function well, but it should be recognised that there are times when they function even better when given some support.

depressive personality

The person suffering from the personality disorder known as the *depressive personality* is very easily recognised, but very difficult to define. He is the sort of person who is perpetually gloomy and pessimistic, for whom defeat is always a likelihood, and whose life is one that never seems to go well. Often such people have a good deal of insight and may even make wryly humorous remarks about themselves. It is quite common for them to be hypochondriacal and always to be on the look-out for a new form of patent medicine to produce some wonder cure. However, they can at times irritate people by their self-pitying attitudes, which can be very wearing indeed.

case 2 Mr Hobbs

Mr Hobbs, aged 30 and unmarried, was a messenger for a large firm of importers. His daily tasks included delivering small packages to various firms around the dockside area in Liverpool. In appearance he was small. He was almost humourless and was rarely seen to smile. He had no close friends, but one of his consuming interests was to play cricket and he was able to join a small cricket club where players were hard to get.

At work, he was known as 'Mr Glum' because of his pessimistic views about everything. On the occasions when he had to deliver a package to a ship, he would always say before he left – 'I'll bet it sails before I get there'. He always gave the impression that he really meant this. Even at cricket, he tried seemingly to convince his team mates that they'd lose before the game started.

When he first joined the cricket club and was asked where he liked to field he said 'in the slips'. However, it soon became apparent that his reactions were far too slow for such a 'close to the wicket' position, with the result that he dropped the catches which were offered. Even more noticeable was the drastic effect that a dropped catch had on him. He would hang his head and be disconsolate despite the sympathy of his team-mates.

His whole life pattern was of this order and there were even occasions when he developed a mild depressive illness especially in the face of some abnormal (for him) stress.

As we pointed out in our preamble to this case, it is a hard picture to define but it is very easily recognised. It should be noted how poorly a man like Mr Hobbs copes with crises and how he tends to retreat from difficult situations, rather than make decisions or take other forms of action. Even Mr Hobbs's job was of a very mundane and non-threatening nature, but even so, he could see nothing but gloom ahead.

The reader will have noticed that many of the signs and symptoms shown by Mr Hobbs were not very dissimilar from a person suffering from a mild depressive illness. *It is important that the two are not confused, particularly because of the risk of suicide which is inherent in the latter.*

the obsessional personality

In Chapter 3 we discussed the main features of an obsessional neurosis. We suggested there that this is not infrequently developed from the *obsessional personality*.

In the development of young children, there is an obsessional stage which is quite normal, but in some instances the child does not fully outgrow the features of this stage and is left with obvious obsessional traits. We pointed out also that many of these retained traits are not only regarded as normal, but may even be desirable for some occupations – for example, tidiness, punctuality and self-discipline. We all know how, during the obsessional stage, children develop little rituals such as walking on the cracks of the pavements, lest some calamity befall them. With an *obsessional personality*, it is frequently this magical element that is retained. Persons who retain it are often prone to indulge in superstitious beliefs and ritual practices; for example, believing that touching wood or some other ritual will enable him to avoid disaster.

case 3 Mr Ames
Mr Ames, aged 40, was a married man with two children. He had his own watch-repairing business. At home, he was a good father and husband and was always helping his wife to tidy the house. There were times however when his insistence on tidiness in the house meant a certain amount of discomfort for his family, who never really felt free to relax completely.

Before setting up his own business, Mr Ames had worked with a precision instrument manufacturing company, but found it difficult to accept some of the bawdy repartee of his workmates. Being a rigid perfectionist, he also found it difficult to work alongside people whose standards were less exact than his own. There were times when he would have dearly liked to tell off a workmate, but he could never bring himself to express his anger.

He led a rather dull, uneventful life and even when on holiday he would deny himself many pleasures (and therefore also his family) because he regarded frivolous spending as sinful.

This is a fairly typical picture of the *obsessional personality*, although sometimes such people develop periods of depression because things affect them so deeply.

Classically, Mr Ames shows many of the perfectionist tendencies that are highly regarded by society and which are necessary for some occupations – in his case, working with fine instruments and within fine limits. Mr Ames also typifies a rigidity of temperament which is not uncommon and which produces a tendency to be over-conformist. He displayed, too, his inability to adapt readily to changes by having to leave a job which he liked and by risking his capital rather than adapting to his work surroundings.

hysterical personality

Most adults are capable of behaving in a rather childish manner when they are sufficiently frustrated and this type of behaviour tends to increase in the presence of tiredness or mental strain. However, generally, the adult's behaviour is appropriate to the situation and the average person is perfectly able to tolerate a reasonable degree of uncertainty and anxiety.

Individuals with *hysterical personalities* appear not to have developed a well-integrated personality and because of this they are frequently unstable and unreliable. On the surface, they usually seem to be quite normal, but in the face of frustration, their tolerance level is seen to be noticeably limited and they tend to over-react to every minor crisis which comes along. Sometimes, such people could be classified as being 'immature' because much of their symptomatology is characteristic of this descriptive term. With the hysterical personality, there is much of the childish behaviour which may remind one of the dementing old person described in the last chapter.

case 4 Miss Chapman

Miss Chapman, aged 27, was a kennel maid and had worked in this employment since she left school at the age of 15. Her father, a merchant seaman, had throughout her life spent long periods away from home. Her mother, rather bored by having only one child to look after, took a full-time job when Miss Chapman was three years old. Her mother tended to show her daughter off rather like a doll instead of a real child, and father, on his rare visits home, fussed over her and demanded kissing and cuddling to show that she loved him. By the time she entered school, it was noticeable that she always wanted to do things for the teacher, was first to volunteer to recite poetry and generally pushed herself forward when given the slightest opportunity.

As a teenager, she displayed a somewhat superficial personality, having no friends of long-standing. In other words, she flitted from one person to another rather like a butterfly. Although her friendships were superficial, she would always swear undying friendship to people whom she had only just met. In return, they felt this to be a bit overwhelming and tended to shy away from her dramatic overtures. She was a very emotional girl, who laughed and cried easily but inconsistently.

In addition to her positive, undying-allegiance approach, she frequently, in her attempts to get attention, alternated this with badgering, sulks, temper tantrums and on one occasion, when she felt she had been jilted, she produced a very superficial attempt at suicide. She took four aspirins, but in her 'death scene' said that she had taken a whole bottle-full.

Throughout her life, she had been extremely fond of animals and as a youngster would dress up her dog in little clothes. It came as no surprise, when on leaving school, she chose to be a kennel maid.

She had many superficial and short-lived attachments to the opposite sex, who found her extremely attractive in the short term, but later realised how sadly lacking in warmth she was. In fact, she found physical contact with men repugnant.

This is a fairly typical picture of the *hysterical personality*, in that there were lavish displays of emotion of a superficial or shallow and inconsistent nature. As is fairly common, she made a great show of immediate warmth, but underneath this she was emotionally infantile and rather frigid. This type of personality is much more common in women than it is in men. When they marry, they not infrequently become 'professional' martyrs, or invalids, who dramatise their inability to sustain their sex relationships by maintaining that their husbands are 'filthy beasts' with 'unnatural sexual appetites.' They may opt out of such relationships by becoming invalids. Despite these common sexual difficulties, some hysterical personalities sometimes become mothers. When they do, they are frequently over-possessive and go to great lengths to retain their children's affections exclusively for themselves. At the same time, they proclaim themselves to be good mothers although, in emotional terms, they undoubtedly 'take' more than they 'give.'

Hysterical personalities frequently provoke disapproval from those about them. This is unfortunate, especially if the person concerned is merely ineffectual, or immature, and does not possess the urge to manipulate people and situations of the true hysterical personality.

It is hardly surprising that people who so earnestly seek attention sometimes find a useful place in society by turning to the stage, where they do well for just so long as they have public acclaim. When they fall from favour and things go wrong, they frequently become anxious and break down completely.

In severe cases of hysterical personality, the disorder can take other forms of psychiatric abnormality such as psychopathy (which will be referred to later in this chapter), or assume other types of antisocial behaviour such as pathological lying, or confidence trickery.

cyclothymic personality

Most of us experience swings of mood, but these are usually not too severe and are very transient. There are some people, however, who become either unduly elated or depressed without any obvious reason; they are said to have a cyclothymic or *cycloid personality*. They are so called because their excessive mood-swings have a tendency to occur in regular cycles. Frequently, such people are called 'moody' because they are so changeable. Unfortunately, it is the depressive, irritable stage that is remembered, rather than the infectiously gay one. When a swing reaches a severe stage there is an excessive tendency for a manic depressive illness to develop (see Chapter 4).

case 5 Mr Walker

Mr Walker, aged 45 was a factory worker, married with no children. He caused a great deal of perplexity amongst his workmates, because they never quite knew how to take him. Some days he would arrive at work 'full of the joys of spring' and engage everyone in lighthearted talk and banter. On these occasions he would be very energetic and his work production would be high. Then, just as quickly, his mood would alter for no apparent reason and he would become surly, rude and uncommunicative. His colleagues would often wonder what they had done to offend him. During such a phase, his work rate would fall and he tended also to be rather careless in his performance.

A member of the local working men's club, he enjoyed playing darts and was rather good at it. However, he frequently let the team down by simply not appearing when he was in one of his low moods.

Mr Walker's picture typifies the person with a *cycloid personality* and shows how difficult they can be to live with. There is some indication that perhaps genetic inheritance plays a part in the development of such a personality, since it is found fairly frequently that parents who show these symptoms have children who subsequently develop manic-depressive illnesses.

schizoid personality

In the same way that a relationship exists between the *cycloid personality* and the development of a manic-depressive illness, so it is with the *schizoid personality* who is not infrequently to be found in the families of schizephrenics. This type of personality quite frequently also develops a schizophrenic illness. However, it should equally be emphasised that many so-called *schizoid personalities* will never develop into schizophrenics. Once again, there is some evidence for the involvement of a genetic inheritance.

case 6 Mr Worthington

Mr Worthington, aged 20, was an architectural student who went to see a student counsellor in the University Health centre complaining about his inability to make friends — particularly with girls.

The counsellor found him to be a shy and aloof young man, who appeared to spend most of his time avoiding contact with his fellows. In the course of his interviews he claimed to be ill at ease at social functions and admitted that he was much happier on his own, reading or listening to records. His whole life style had been almost hermit-like and singularly lacking in human intercourse. He was a very humourless young man, who resented any form of criticism levelled at him, however constructive. He tended to brood over such happenings and to magnify their significance.

There was no doubt that his behaviour was very a-social

and that, despite his youth, he was regarded by the people around him as something of a crank, particularly since his sole social contact was to belong to a small sect devoted to the study of black magic.

During several interviews with the counsellor he had great difficulty in expressing emotion and tended always to turn conversations into areas of his own interest, rather than to talk about himself as a person. Indeed, the counselling service could not effect any change in him, because he withdrew from it after only four sessions.

It was of interest that, when he did talk about his family, he presented his mother as a rather cold and unsympathetic person, from whom he gained little emotional warmth.

As the result of possessing such personality traits the schizoid individual frequently remains unmarried. This, of course, tends to increase the isolated nature of his existence. However, this does not necessarily cause him discomfort, since he has little interest in being with others and no real wish to change his way of life. In spite of this, it may be important to make some social effort to involve such a person in group activities and, perhaps more importantly, to provide support for other members of his family, who may be suffering from the effects of his emotional coldness.

paranoid personality

In many ways the *schizoid personality* is rather like the personality of the case which we now present and which could be categorised as a *paranoid personality*.

case 7 Mr Hood

Mr Hood was a single man in his mid-thirties with a poor work record, normally employed as an unskilled labourer. Although he had a good circle of acquaintances they rarely became friends, because of his extreme touchiness and his feelings that at times he was being deliberately victimised by them. Indeed, he explained his many changes of work in this way and also suggested that his lack of success was the result of malice on the part of others.

He maintained that, because his nose was somewhat prominent this turned many people against him, as they did not like his looks. At other times, he attributed his job losses to the fact that he was more skilled than the foremen, who resented this. Many of his evenings were spent in pubs, where he complained endlessly about the supposed wrongs he had suffered, to anyone who would listen. He would tell them how he would like to put these to rights, but in fact never did anything about them.

We have shown Mr Hood to be a rather sensitive, suspicious and ineffectual character. Such sensitivity is often confused with shyness, but shy people are by no means *paranoid personalities*. It is only when symptoms like Mr Hood's cluster together that such a diagnosis can be made. Not all *paranoid personalities* are ineffectual and many of them make good 'watch dogs' and guardians or promoters of the rights of others, because of their quickness to spot injustices. When kept within these bounds, such people are obviously very useful to have around. However, when they become litigious and drag innumerable cases through the courts they can become nuisances, because they can never accept legal defeat and always maintain that they have been the subject of a miscarriage of justice when things go against them. Sometimes, people with a personality of this nature become chronic hypochondriacs, who complain of having very serious illnesses but who lack sufficient insight to realise that, if the illnesses complained of were real, they would have been dead long ago.

case 8 Mr Carver

Mr Carver, aged 38, was an unusually young managing director of a large international firm. He was seen by his staff to be totally unapproachable and lacking in any kind of emotional warmth. He achieved his high position because of his tremendous drive and undoubted ability, which he harnessed to reach his goals no matter who or what stood in his way. Indeed, many of his own colleagues were the victims of his rapid progress as he trampled over them to get to the top. Despite the many casualties that he caused, he would shrug his shoulders and maintain that if they weren't 'good enough' they were there to be got rid of.

Mr Carver came to the notice of a psychiatrist in private practice, whom he had consulted because he himself had become a victim of the 'rat race'. He told the psychiatrist that he had been unjustly asked to leave by his board of directors, because they were a group of 'old women' who disliked 'straight talking'. In fact, he had lost his job because of a very ill-considered business venture, which he had pursued in defiance of the finance director and which had cost the company a great deal of money.

It is of interest to note that by the age of 38 Mr Carver had been married and divorced twice. In both instances, because of his inability to have anything other than a 'veneer-type' of relationship with his two wives, they were unable to tolerate the cloak of respectability which appeared to be the sole reason for the marriages.

In his early life, there was evidence of severe emotional deprivation by his parents. Indeed, so cruel were they to him, that he had been removed from home to the care of the local authority when only four years old.

The psychiatrist was quite unable to effect any change in Mr Carver's attitudes in the treatment sessions. He was completely unmoved by references to the possible distress that he might have caused to others.

affectionless personality

This type of case is probably a sub-category of psychopathy, but differs largely because it does not necessarily produce antisocial behaviour of a kind that conflicts with the law. The personality displayed by Mr Carver is referred to as that of the *affectionless personality*. The reader will have noted that in some senses he is quite like the *schizoid personality*, but he lacks *all* evidence of the presence of any finer feelings.

psychopathy

The types of personality abnormalities which have been presented thus far can be seen as illnesses or inadequacies, which are fairly readily recognised as such, especially in their more severe forms. The patient or sufferer is often very tense and extremely unhappy. Because of his abnormality, he is denied the pleasures of normal social intercourse. The abnormality which we are now about to present, however, is a condition in which the individual usually appears to suffer very little, but frequently causes suffering to all those around him. The *psychopath*, to use the term normally given to this extreme end of the personality disorder spectrum, is usually not just asocial, but is often actually antisocial. Indeed, so often does he clash with society that frequently he is called a *sociopath*.

case 9 Mr Wilcox

Mr Wilcox, aged 29, was admitted to the casualty ward of a general hospital following an attempt at suicide. His immediate story was that he had behaved in this dangerous manner because his wife and two young children had just left him and had returned to her mother.

It soon became clear that this was not the whole story, when a policeman appeared at the hospital to question him. Apparently his wife had not left him recently – but had in fact done so some time earlier. He had pestered his mother-in-law and had forcibly entered her house to remove his family on several previous occasions. At the time of his suicide attempt he was in breach of a court order which restrained him from seeing his wife. During this breach, he had violently attacked his wife and his parents-in-law and had run away when neighbours were known to have gone for the police.

His early history was one of severe deprivation, although both his parents lived in the same house. His mother was a lady of leisure and his father an habitual criminal. Mr Wilcox was a fairly intelligent young man who recounted with pleasure how his parents had rewarded him with money when he produced a good school report. When the reports were bad, he shamelessly admitted that from the age of 8 he had signed them himself.

To cut the story short, Mr Wilcox presented a long history of delinquency, having graduated from probation to approved school and thence to Borstal. At the time of his admission he had spent twelve periods in prison. He had also been hospitalised for gastric surgery, after which his sexual appetite, normally very high, became totally insatiable and deviant. Indeed, it was for this reason, on top of his normal brutality towards his wife, that the break in the marriage occurred.

Needless to say, he had a shocking work record, having been frequently fired for theft, bad time-keeping, insubordination and assault. His last prison sentence, which had been some two years earlier, had been occasioned by theft and hire purchase swindling, in order to furnish his new council house. His last job had been as a bookie's runner but he had lost this job because of an elaborate attempt to swindle his employer.

When interviewed after he had physically recovered, he immediately demanded of the psychiatrist and the social worker that they fetch the wife back . . . 'Otherwise I'll make a real job of it next time . . .'

case 10 Mr Harvey
Mr Harvey was a middle-aged man who stopped to talk to an elderly lady who was working in her front garden. He commented that she could be doing with a new gate. When the old lady agreed to this, he said he would return in a day or two to fit it for her. True to his word, the gate was fitted in a couple of days and a fairly exorbitant price charged. He had been 'such a nice man' that no price had been agreed prior to acceptance of his offer. On the day the gate was fitted, another man was seen to be examining it rather closely. When she questioned him about this, he introduced himself as a police inspector and informed her that his own gate had been stolen a day earlier and that her new gate was his.

On hearing the old lady's description of Mr Harvey, the police officer smiled and said that he knew who the man was. However, he was glad to have the opportunity to visit him at his home, since he suspected there would be much more to be found there that had been acquired dishonestly. And so it proved to be.

Both these cases show some of the irrational behaviour that frequently causes people to believe that the psychopath is intellectually retarded. In fact, mental retardation is certainly not one of the main diagnostic features. There are some dull psychopaths, but the majority are of normal intelligence. They often present, like Mr Harvey, as normal, pleasant people and this frequently lulls others into a sense of false security. Both the cases have in common an obvious lack of both insight and foresight. Both also show a total disregard for other people and an inability to control their impulses.

If such people become patients, as did Mr Wilcox, they will co-operate for just so long as it suits them, but whenever things become too tedious or temptation appears, they will quickly revert to their habitual pattern of self centredness or criminality.

'No matter how normal his appearance and behaviour appear on the surface, the individual with a severely *psychopathic personality* is one of the most abnormal in the community and with his aggressiveness and lack of any moral sensibility he can also be one of the most dangerous;' (Munro and McCulloch, 1969). Given this, it is hardly surprising to find that such behaviour, which is not psychotic, fools many inexperienced people into refusing to believe that such an apparently average person can be so utterly unreliable and prone to crime as many psychopaths are.

Mr Wilcox's case typifies the kind of early environmental experiences which appear to breed this type of personality. Both cases typify the inadequate psychopath, but many criminal masterminds, who show basically the same traits, are extremely adequate in their ability to plan robberies and other crimes on a large scale. One other major feature which is obvious in psychopathy is impulsivity – they want things when they want them and are not prepared to delay gratification. This aspect is particularly demonstrated by Mr Wilcox's efforts to furnish his house. One of the difficulties incurred with the psychopath is his total resistance to any known forms of treatment, though there is evidence that some psychopaths lose much of their aggressiveness and impulsivity with advancing years.

psychosexual disorders

In all the illnesses described in this book so far, there can be deviations from the normal in sexual functioning. We have, for example, described the frigidity of the hysterical personality, the uncontrolled and insatiable sexual impulses of some psychopaths and the fall-off in sexual drive frequently associated with a depressive illness. It is not our intention to give case examples of the other sexual disorders, but only to mention briefly what they entail. We would caution the reader to be very careful in deciding what is abnormal and what is not in sexual relationships, since there is a very wide variation in sexual attitudes and practices amongst 'normal' people. As in the case of the personality disorders, we will refer only to the extremes, although some of these are more and more becoming acceptable by society.

masturbation

Although this used to be regarded as a sign of moral degeneracy and was thought to produce insanity, it is, in fact, a normal habit, particularly during adolescence. Indeed, some people continue with self-stimulation throughout their adult lives. It is important to understand that masturbation is *not* a cause of mental illness, although over-indulgence frequently indicates solitariness and isolation and, for some people, even perhaps a retreat from reality. It is really only in the minority of cases that masturbation is a sign of some deeper disturbance.

impotence

Potency should not be confused with fertility, since some very potent males are infertile and impotent ones fertile. Basically, impotence is the inability to achieve and sustain penile erection in order to complete the sexual act. It can arise from a variety of causes. It may be that there is a lack of sexual desire. This, for some people, can be a permanent state due to a failure of psychological development. It can also be due to a temporary state of exhaustion, depressive illness, anxiety, or an unsatisfactory relationship with the sexual partner.

It is encouraging to find that there is a growth in the number of agencies offering specialised help for this particular problem. These include Marriage Guidance Councils, Family Planning Organisations and Sex Clinics.

frigidity

This is the female equivalent to impotence. In this condition, women consistently fail to achieve sexual satisfaction during intercourse. It is relatively common and a great number of women are totally unaware that they are missing a fulfilling experience, because they have not had an orgasm at any time. Frigidity is a wide term and there are varying degrees of it, but the complete form is usually associated with marked psychosexual immaturity (as was evidenced in the case of Miss Webster). In lesser degrees of frigidity, there may be many reasons for its presence; in some cases it is due entirely to the clumsiness of the sexual partner, but it can also be due to a fear of pregnancy, a lack of privacy, or to unconscious lesbian (homosexual) tendencies. It may also be due, as we have seen, to a depressive illness.

homosexuality (male and female)

It is quite normal for both males and females to go through a stage in adolescence when their sexual emotions become increased in intensity, but are not yet properly orientated. It is during this period that 'crushes' on members of the same sex are common. In the same period, or even earlier, there is a certain amount of sexual experimentation with members of the same sex, just because they are there and equally sexually curious. When the orientation of sex has been completed and remains fixed on a member of the same sex, then one can say that homosexuality exists. It is fairly common in the western world and it has been estimated that upwards of five per cent of adult males are practising homosexuals. There cannot be a similar estimate for female homosexuals (lesbians), since they tend to be content to keep their homosexual inclinations hidden from the general public and they are probably only made dramatically overt by the female psychopath, who likes to make a show of her abnormality.

The above are the commonest sexual disorders but there are some others which are less common and which we shall now briefly mention.

sado-masochism

This is when sexual enjoyment is obtained from the infliction of physical or mental pain (sadism), or from the receipt of hurt or humiliation (masochism). The general tendency is for men to be sadistic and women masochistic, but exceptions are known.

voyeurism

This is a form of behaviour in which sexual pleasure is gained by surreptitiously 'peeping' at naked people or by 'peeping' in the hope of finding naked persons indulging in sexual behaviour. It is often suggested that the 'peeping' itself additionally provides pleasure of a quasi-sexual nature, because of the possibility of being caught in the act.

transvestism
This is when sexual pleasure is derived from dressing in the clothes of the opposite sex. Despite the fantasies associated with transvestism, many of its practitioners are in fact heterosexual.

exhibitionism
This occurs when a man exposes his genitalia to a woman or to a child, in the hope that it will sexually stimulate them – which it rarely does. However, the fear or disgust expressed by the victims frequently produce orgasm for the exhibitionist.

We are conscious of dealing very superficially with the psychosexual disorders, but this is partly because they are to be dealt with in detail elsewhere in this series. In addition, we did not wish to elaborate unduly upon these disorders as illnesses in their own right, since they can manifest themselves at any place in the *continuum* from the normal to the grossly abnormal personality.

reference
Munro, A., and McCulloch, W. *Psychiatry for Social Workers*. Pergamon. Oxford, 1969.

recommended reading
Cleckly, H. *The Mask of Sanity*. C. V. Mosley. St Louis, 1941.

7 The problems of drugs and alcohol

Before we deal individually with the problems associated with drugs and alcohol, it is important to say something about the word addiction. There is some reason for suggesting that addiction is a rather over-used word, which may perhaps obscure rather than clarify. More and more the word 'dependence,' which is more descriptive, is being introduced into the literature.

'Excessive use of chemicals is not unique to any particular society, though it is true that the type of chemicals used may vary from community to community, and within the same community from time to time. For example, alcohol, hypnotics and amphetamines are more widely misused in materially affluent communities like those of the West, than are opiates and cannabis, which find favour among the materially not-so-developed countries of South East Asia and the Middle East. None the less, noticeable use of the opiates and hallucingenic drugs like cannabis or L.S.D. has developed in the last ten years in the United Kingdom.' (Rathod.)

It is difficult to be definitive as to the quantity of a drug, or the time that it takes, in order to produce a state of dependence. In the case of some narcotic drugs, constant usage over a period of just a few weeks could create dependence, whereas it might take months in the case of barbiturates and sometimes years in the case of alcohol. We would wish to emphasise that occasional use of drugs does not necessarily lead to dependence. So far as drugs are concerned, the World Health Organisation Expert Committee (1964) has suggested that the word 'addiction' be abandoned and be replaced by the term we have mentioned, 'dependence.' They recognise five distinct drug types: morphine and its equivalents, barbiturates, cocaine, amphetamines and cannabis. Alcohol was not included in this Committee's terms of reference.

The characteristics of dependence were defined by W.H.O. as follows:

(1) Whether or not there is a strong desire or need for the drug.

(2) Whether or not the user acquires 'tolerance' to the drug and therefore needs to increase the dose.

(3) Whether or not there is a psychic dependence on the effects of the drug related to subjective and individual appreciation of those effects.

(4) Whether or not there is physical dependence on the drug, so that its presence is required for the maintenance of homeostasis (i.e. to keep the user in the same state), and an abstinence syndrome develops.

There is at least one basic difference between those who are dependent on drugs and those who are dependent on alcohol. Whereas, in the former, dependence is accompanied by a need for increased dosage, in the latter this is a transient feature, since the alcoholic, in the later stages of his progress, tends to have a diminished tolerance.

drug dependence

We do not propose to give a lengthy account of this problem but rather to describe what we see as its essentials. Those readers wishing to pursue the subject further are recommended to consider the literature listed at the end of this chapter.

'A part of this increased (drug problem) complexity is related to the great scientific advances in the field of pharmacology in the last fifty years. Today we have at our disposal drugs that literally cover the whole spectrum of human behaviour. Besides 'the Pill,' we have pills to sedate us when we are nervous, excite us when we are dull, slim us when we are fat, fatten us when we are thin, waken us when we are sleepy, put us to sleep when we are awake, cure us when we are sick and make us sick when we are well! Drugs can enhance our ability to function, and they can carry our minds out of the realm of reality into loneliness.' (Glatt *et al.*, 1967.)

As is shown by the above quotation, drugs of various sorts are part of everyday life and the majority of people now believe that there is a tablet for every ill. Not only this, but people are tending, as many general practitioners attest, to have more and more frequent recourse to drugs.

'In present day Great Britain, several million adults regularly take sleeping tablets and one estimate has suggested that possibly two million people are habituated to them. Most of these individuals would vehemently deny that they are virtually drug addicts, and it is true that in most cases the dependence is psychological.' (Munro and McCulloch, 1969.)

By habituation is meant simply 'habit formation.' Most of us have formed a habit for taking something, perhaps the most common substance being tobacco. We would point out that although a drug may be habit-forming, that is not necessarily the cause of dependence upon it. However, there is no doubt that all drugs which cause dependence are also habit-forming.

common drugs used

We give below a short list of the drugs which tend to be misused. By 'misused' we mean that the drugs have been acquired illegally, or are those which have been acquired legally, but where the dosage is beyond that of normal requirements.

(a) amphetamines. These are commonly known as 'black bombers' or 'black and tans.' They are packed in capsule form but were previously marketed as tablets and were then known as 'purple hearts' or 'French Blues.' These drugs are almost invariably swallowed and their effects consist mainly of a stimulation of the central nervous system. People who use this drug moderately tend to become talkative, excited or elated, but heavy usage sometimes produces irritability, aggressive behaviour and, on occasion, paranoia (see Chapter 4). Frequently the user will have shaking hands, will sweat profusely and his pupils will be dilated. The aftermath of the use of these drugs is extreme tiredness and depression and this feeling induces the individual to take ever-increasing amounts. The amphetamines produce psychological, rather than physical, dependence. It has been estimated that somewhere in the region of twenty per cent, or above, of people who use them will become habituated. Fortunately, they have now become very much more difficult than before to obtain.

(b) **barbiturates.** These are sedative drugs and there are many varieties of them, but the family is colloquially known by the nicknames 'goof balls,' 'barbs,' or 'sleepers.' The effects of these drugs range from mild sedation to complete coma and the early effects of a large dose are not unlike drunkenness – slurred speech, dilated pupils, poor judgment etc. Occasionally, over-usage of this drug produces irritability, depression and even suicidal tendencies. As with alcohol, driving after the use of barbiturates is extremely hazardous for both the user and the public. According to the World Health Organisation, these are drugs which cause dependence because there is a craving to continue with them, a need to increase the dosage and psychic and physical dependence, which results in withdrawal problems when the drug is withheld. The main source of supply in Britain is probably the National Health Service and it is estimated that about 1,200 people in every 100,000 who use this drug abuse it.

(c) **L.S.D.** This is a hallucinogenic drug which is supplied as a colourless, tasteless, odourless liquid or as an off-white powder, a small white pill and more recently as a capsule. The slang names for the capsules are 'cherry-top,' 'purple haze,' or 'blue cheer.' For the other forms the common parlance is 'acid,' 'instant Zen,' 'hock,' 'chief,' or 'sugar.' Although this drug is totally prohibited, its use in the United Kingdom has spread in recent years and the penalties for its possession are quite high. There are variations in the effects of the use of this drug, which make it more dangerous than some others. In the jargon, there can be good 'trips' and there can be very bad ones; some users experience dilation of the pupils, hand shaking, sweaty palms, flushed face, shivering, loss of appetite and nausea. Usually a 'trip' produces bizarre mental reactions and distortion of the physical senses. It can sometimes build up a paranoid state which can last for quite a time and, under its influence, some users have killed themselves by misinterpreting reality; for example, trying to pick up a moving bus. One of the most unfortunate effects of this drug is that its hallucinations may come weeks after it has been taken and this causes the user to feel that he is going insane. It is not physically addicting, although repeated use tends to diminish its effects.

(d) cannabis. This drug is also hallucinogenic and is commonly referred to as 'Mary Jane,' 'grass,' 'pot,' 'tea,' 'weed,' 'Texas tea' etc. Most commonly it is smoked, but it can also be put into soft drinks or into sweets or cakes. It causes dilation of the pupils, reddening of the eyes, increased appetite, a craving for sugar and it increases the urge to urinate. It can cause the user to become dizzy and nauseated. Generally, the use of cannabis reduces inhibitions and it also slightly impairs judgment and memory, distorts perception and sensation and frequently increases the sexual urge. Mood changes are common, and the user frequently becomes incongruously hilarious or loquacious, but at times the change is towards depression, apprehension and even panic. The effects begin within minutes of smoking and last up to about four hours, according to the dosage. Not infrequently, the constant use of cannabis causes lethargy and self-neglect. The user is often deluded by false feelings of increased capability and, equally frequently, becomes depressed by the consequent disappointments caused by the gap between what he thinks he can do and what he actually achieves.

This drug produces psychological dependence because it stimulates a desire for continued use, but there is no physical dependence.

(e) opiates. Heroin is the major drug in this group and, like its main companion, morphine, is characterised by a very speedy onset of dependence, both psychological and physical. The major symptoms displayed by the user are running eyes and nose, general aches, restlessness and alternate hot and cold flushes. The more severe symptoms are high fever, loss of appetite, weight loss, dehydration, sleeplessness, heavy perspiration, nausea, vomiting, cramps and diarrhoea. It is estimated that there may be more than four thousand illegal users in the United Kingdom. The penalties for misuse can be very high; even more so for trafficking, which can bring a prison sentence of up to fourteen years. People who become 'hooked' on these drugs have a very short life expectation and the suicide rate is *very* high.

the people who take drugs. The largest group are young people between the ages of sixteen and twenty-five and there are more men than women. Frequently, young people are introduced to the drug scene by being offered a pill, or a smoke, at a party at which there are people who are already drug misusers. In the main, drug takers tend to be rather solitary people, or to be immature or unstable. Sometimes, a lack of confidence is the thing that prompts them to turn to drugs for a 'boost.' At other times, drugs are started as a form of escape from some form of personal crisis. Perhaps the most dangerous introduction is the result of surreptitious 'pushing.'

Another major group of drug misusers are those people who have been introduced to them for medical reasons and whose treatment has been continued too long. Unfortunately, this is not simply confined to patients, for doctors, nurses and others who work in the medical field are somewhat vulnerable because of their easier access to drugs. There is also a group of drug users consisting of people with *personality disorders* (particularly psychopaths) (see Chapter 6). Generally, these are people who, as we had pointed out, have difficulty in coping with personal and social problems. Because of their anti-social feelings and the difficulties they have in fitting into normal life, many of them turn to drugs or alcohol, or both.

We shall now present a few cases which illustrate the misuse of drugs.

case 1 Miss Croft

Miss Croft was a sixteen-year-old, intelligent, student from a materially good home background. She was an only child and therefore all her associations and companionships tended to be with her peer group. A girl friend of long standing took her to a 'discotheque' where they joined a large group of teenagers. During the evening, she was introduced to amphetamines. Since she normally stayed with her girl friend on the evenings they went out together, her parents were not able to spot the 'hang-over' which ensued after this event, and unfortunately, after many others in the weeks that followed.

After a fairly short period of about six months, she was so dependent that she was easily recruited as a 'pusher' and also as a drug thief. Her inexperience as the latter ensured that she was quickly caught by the police. However, as a first offender, the court took a lenient view and placed her on probation with a requirement that she received medical treatment.

With a great deal of difficulty the probation officer and the doctor were able to wean her away from the group she had been mixing with and as a consequence from the drugs also. When the parents were first acquainted with the facts about their daughter they just could not believe them and claimed, even at the stage of arrest by the police, that she was more 'sinned against then sinning', despite the fact that she had also been charged with 'pushing'. A great deal of work was required to help the parents understand the pressures which their daughter had been facing and there were many difficulties before the case was satisfactorily concluded.

case 2 Mr Holt

Mr Holt was a nineteen-year-old youth, the second of six children. He came from a very unhappy home background, characterised by parental disharmony and physical abuse. At school he was a disappointment and frequently truanted. During these absences from school he was apprehended for shoplifting and other offences. As a result of this behaviour he had been to Approved School and Borstal and was therefore known to the local police. Because he was so well-known he was comparatively easily spotted when he began to frequent public places which were associated with the drug scene, although he was never charged with any drug offence. He came to medical attention because he appeared to have developed a paranoid illness. (In the event this proved to be the aftermath of drug abuse.) This resulted in his being hospitalised. The history of his drug taking was as follows:

He was introduced to drugs at the age of 15 by users who frequented a local café, first to cannabis which he smoked daily thereafter, and then to L.S.D., which he began to take three or four times each week. By the time he was 17 he had begun to take cocaine, but his major drug remained L.S.D. Some weeks after his admission to hospital he became aurally and visually hallucinated, despite the fact that his last L.S.D. 'trip' had been before his admission. The major diagnosis made in his case was 'drug dependence in a psychopathic personality'.

case 3 Mr Bass

Mr Bass was a twenty-year-old, highly intelligent student of modern languages. The eldest of four children, he had always been a very introspective person. He maintained that he started to take cannabis as an intellectual experience and said that he had decided that it was quite harmless.

Information from his tutor indicated that there had been a falling off in his work, despite the fact that Mr Bass was apparently more confident about his ability than his performance warranted. The tutor also noticed that Mr Bass's personal appearance had deteriorated very considerably, but had assumed that this was no more than being part of a 'student cult'. This information coincided exactly with the beginning of Mr Bass's drug taking.

Because of the enormous disappointment Mr Bass experienced when he failed his examination for the first time ever, he became mildly depressed and sought the help of the student counselling service.

Fortunately, treatment was effective and Mr Bass completed his degree course without any further difficulties.

case 4 Mrs Harper

Mrs Harper was a married woman whose marital relationships could only be described as disastrous. She had been married previously and this marriage had ended in divorce. Her early history had been marked by severe emotional deprivation.

Mrs Harper had initially been prescribed barbiturates many

years earlier, following her divorce, because she had been suffering from insomnia. More and more she became dependent on these drugs until she could not get to sleep without increasing the dose. Her G.P. wisely curtailed her prescriptions because of her ever-increasing requests for more tablets. This resulted in a series of changes of doctor, in order to fulfil her needs for more and more drugs. She also admitted having obtained barbiturates illicitly. She was admitted to hospital after a neighbour had found her sitting slumped over her dining-room table in a stuporous condition. The neighbour said that she should have spotted the over-use of drugs sooner, but thought that Mrs Harper had been 'imbibing' too freely.

Throughout the investigations, Mrs. Harper said that she was not addicted, but that she 'just couldn't get to sleep', or go through a day without drugs.

case 5 Mr Long

Mr Long was aged 19 but had already been married and divorced. At the age of 16 he had been arrested and charged with a cannabis offence and less than a year later had begun to take heroin and became a regular user. Unfortunately, in addition to his legal supply as a registered addict, he was also able to procure heroin, cocaine and other drugs illegally. This was an intelligent young man from a seemingly secure home background although he had tended to be over-indulged fairly considerably. After it became known to his parents that he was taking 'main line drugs' they rejected him completely and he committed suicide shortly afterwards.

These cases have in common an aura of tragedy and suffering, not only for the drug taker but in many instances for his family and others close to him. They demonstrate broken careers and shattered dreams. All the cases typify noticeably the remarks we made earlier in the chapter when we described briefly the various drugs which are commonly misused.

It is widely maintained that the use of cannabis is comparatively harmless, but the present authors feel very strongly that there is insufficient knowledge about the short- and long-term effect of the drug to warrant such complacency. Like alcohol, the consumer never knows at the start whether or not he is likely to become dependent, or to move to stronger drugs, just as in much the same way the social beer drinker may move on to spirits.

We would recommend most strongly that, if parents or other guardians of the young have reason to believe that those for whom they have a responsibility are taking drugs, they should quickly seek expert guidance. This is not to suggest that we should follow our children's every move with apprehension, since this may merely lead to mistrust and misunderstanding. But when it has been established that drugs have been taken it is worth noting Mitchell's recommendations for help in such crisis situations. These are: 'Have a cooling off period: keep a sense of perspective; keep a sense of humour: and know who to turn to for help.'

alcohol

The World Health Organisation defines alcoholics as 'those excessive drinkers whose dependence on alcohol has attained such a degree that they show a noticeable mental disturbance or an interference with their mental and bodily health, their inter-personal relations and their smooth social and economic functioning; or who show the prodromal signs of such developments. They therefore require treatment.' (W.H.O. 1952.) We have chosen to begin with this definition so that there will be no subsequent confusion in the reader's mind as to what we mean by the term 'alcoholism.'

The problem of alcoholism is a very large and complex one. It is estimated that in Britain alone there may be as many as 350,000 alcoholics, a quarter of whom show signs of mental and physical deterioration.

In the past, and sometimes today, the alcoholic is considered to be a 'sinful' person, whose cure lies in his own hands – all he has to do is to stop drinking. In fact, we regard alcoholism as a sickness since, even before reaching the stage encompassed by our definition, these are people who can no longer stop their drinking habits even when they want to do so.

Alcoholism is a killing disease and death is commonly caused by cirrhosis of the liver, malnutrition, road accidents and suicide. Indeed, Kessel and Grossman (1961) described alcoholism itself as 'chronic suicide.'

So far as alcohol is concerned, there are five distinct groups of people in any community. (1) Those who never drink at all. (2) The social drinker. (3) The excessive social drinker – such people drink in company and become intoxicated frequently. (4) Alcoholics. (5) Chronic alcoholics – a group which differs from alcoholics in that physical damage has now resulted from their drinking.

In the process of becoming an alcoholic, or a chronic alcoholic, there are various stages that can be identified. Thus, in the stage of pre-alcoholic, excessive drinking mentioned earlier, the drinker tends to spend an increasing amount of time in social drinking and on these occasions he drinks more and more. In the process, he will 'sneak' drinks by buying an extra one for himself when it is his turn to buy the round, or by saying he is going to the toilet and, instead, nipping into the saloon bar for an extra drink. Noticeably in this phase, the drinker tends to become very preoccupied with drinking and with talking about his prowess as a drinker. This is hardly surprising, since at this time there is also an increased tolerance for drink. The drinker often then tends to move over from beer to spirits, even though his companions still drink beer. Very often he drinks in response to tension and when he gets drunk, the following morning he not infrequently suffers from 'boozer's gloom'. In this state, he feels guilty about the previous night's escapade and swears to his wife that he'll never touch another drop, but his resolution is short-lived. More and more, he has to drink so that he can perform adequately at work and to get into the right mood for his social drinking. Drink becomes a necessity, with an accompanying rise in his feelings of guilt.

In the next phase – the addictive phase – the drinker frequently arrives home after a drinking spree and cannot remember how he got there, although he may have done so under his own steam. These *amnestic episodes*, as they are called, increase in frequency and more and more there is a loss of control with regard to drinking, which becomes even more of a compulsion. There is a general reduction of interests, a drop in work efficiency and frequent absenteeism. Drinking takes place now during the day, as well as in the evening. In this phase, the drinking has become a noticeable problem which frequently brings reproof from family and employers. This in turn brings a lowering of self-esteem (and increases the post-drinking remorse) for which he compensates, while among his drinking friends, by his bragging, generosity and financial extravagance.

In the alcoholic phase there is a stepping-up of the addictive element and deceit is practised increasingly in order to prevent discovery. Not surprisingly, by now debts are usually incurred and there is more social isolation. There are occasional aggressive, and sometimes violent, outbursts. If the alcoholic is married, his wife has to take over more and more of the family responsibilities. This, in addition to the friction caused by his drinking, produces great deterioration in marital relations.

Such bad relationships are frequently misinterpretated in a paranoid manner – 'my wife is picking on me' – and this sort of attitude breeds self-pity, which seems to justify his drinking and the accompanying self-deception. There are many other signs of deterioration, such as a reduction in sexual drive, loss of appetite and neglect of eating, morning hand tremors, loss of employment, the hiding of liquor supplies and suicidal impulses and attempts. Frequently, a total break-up of the family occurs during this stage.

In the chronic-alcoholism stage, physical and mental symptoms dominate. Eating becomes almost non-existent and tolerance for alcohol diminishes. There is a switch to cheap wines and even to crude spirits, and the individual displays a total loss of pride and a general deterioration in personal habits. In addition, physical illness and bouts of delirium tremens are common. This latter is characteristic in its symptomatology. There is marked sweating, a reddening of the face, severe tremors affecting the hands and the upper part of the body, and speech is slurred. Visual hallucinations may be present and small animals such as mice, rats, snakes etc. are seen. This is usually accompanied by severe anxiety, or even intense terror. It is in this stage that the chronic alcoholic hears what the Americans would call 'the rustling of goose feathers' and, if he has any sense left, seeks help from medical and other sources, such as Alcoholics Anonymous.

Before proceeding to describe two cases, we would like to make brief reference to what has been said about the wives of some alcoholics. Quite often, the girls who marry alcoholics are older than their husbands, know about his excessive drinking before the marriage and are frequently themselves the daughters of alcoholics. Some of them appear to treat their alcoholic husbands rather like babies. Perhaps this is because they are often very capable people, who have no great need for an adequate husband and who readily combine the paternal with the maternal role. This very often emphasises the alcoholic's own sense of inadequacy to which we referred earlier. When involved in an alcoholic's treatment situation, wives are often tense. They feel that the psychiatrist infers blame, and protest that if any blame is merited then it should be ascribed to the offending husband. In other words, it appears that even the alcoholic's wife finds it difficult to see alcoholism as an illness, or to accept that she has any part to play in it or its treatment. Frequently, the alcoholic's wife will completely opt out of her husband's treatment situation.

case 6 Mr Short

Mr Short, a married man aged 48, went to see his general practitioner about his drinking problem and was subsequently referred to a psychiatrist. It soon became apparent that he had not really come of his own volition, but because his employer had informed him that if he did not seek treatment he would lost his job. Indeed, Mr Short denied vehemently that he was an alcoholic.

He was always a restless, intense person, who never seemed to be able to enjoy himself. He was an extremely hard and conscientious worker in the wine trade, where he was involved perforce in a certain amount of social and business drinking. There were also dinners and dances which he had to attend in connection with his work. In the beginning, he was not averse to dodging some of these, but as time went on he not only attended as many of these functions as he could, but organised parties of his own.

Mr Short, realising the temptations of his trade from the stories that abounded, rarely drank in the middle of the day until some five years before his admission to hospital. At this point, he not only began drinking and entertaining at lunch times, but more and more insisted to his wife (and himself) that this was a necessary part of his work. At this time also Mr Short began to drink more spirits than had been his practice and to have 'sneak' drinks when he was buying rounds for others.

He became well known as a man who could hold his liquor and he did not forget to tell those around him that this was so. This frequently led to bouts of drinking that could only be called 'challenge matches'. These bouts started at lunch time and continued until the last pub closed and always at the expense of his work.

Part of his firm's system of financing entertaining was to provide representatives with a substantial float for expenses. But by now, this came nowhere near to meeting the real costs of his drinking. He reacted to this by telling them that he was entertaining when in fact he was not. In due course this deception was insufficient and he began to retain cash paid to him by customers, by forwarding his personal cheque to his employers. In this way he had the use of his customer's money for three or four days before his own cheque could be cashed. In due course the inevitable happened and his cheque 'bounced'. It was at this point that his employer forced his referral for treatment.

The symptoms outlined earlier in this section were all present, but this case also shows very clearly the process of entanglement and indicates the possible disastrous effects of alcoholism in the social sense. Mr Short's employer, being in the wine trade, was tolerant, but it can be readily appreciated that in other circumstances, not only loss of work would have followed, but quite possibly prosecution. Treatment would also have been delayed. In Mr Short's case, treatment was not successful, as unfortunately it rarely is, unless the alcoholic acknowledges that he is no longer in control of his drinking and seeks treatment without coercion.

case 7 Mr Hunt

Mr Hunt was a man in his late forties, married with a married daughter living away from home. He was the proprietor of his own shop in Manchester. He and his wife lived in accommodation above it.

Mr Hunt was admitted to hospital suffering from delirium tremens and was at a stage when he really wanted help for his drinking. He was prepared to acknowledge that he was an alcoholic. He had gone through, in classical manner, all the stages we outlined earlier.

Mrs Hunt was also the kind of wife we depicted and was a competent business woman. She was perfectly able to run the shop, as she had had to do in the period preceding her husband's admission to hospital, due to the time he had spent away from his work drinking.

Mrs Hunt was not prepared to enter into the treatment session after the first interview with the psychiatrist, but despite this Mr Hunt made good progress and was discharged after about six months. The hospital was one in which it was recognised that patients might have lapses and they were encouraged to 'live for the day'. It was not a 'closed' hospital and any patient could visit a local pub without let or hindrance. During his treatment, Mr Hunt did have one or two lapses early on, but for four months prior to his discharge there were none. While in hospital, there were many activities which interested him, so that by the time his discharge approached he was always occupied.

His reception home was, to say the least of it, cold. His wife patently did not trust him and went so far as to lock him in the flat when she went to work.

Some days later Mr Hunt threw himself out of the window in front of a bus and was killed outright.

While presenting another classic picture of an alcoholic, there is one additional point of great importance to be observed in Mr Hunt's case. As we have said, alcoholics spend a great deal of time drinking at the expense of all other activities. During treatment, their time is often filled with interesting occupation, which, in Mr Hunt's case were totally missing when he went home – especially since he was debarred from even leaving the flat. It is noticeable that quite a considerable number of alcoholics kill themselves shortly after the conclusion of their treatment, and this may well be one of the reasons. Mr Hunt's case also emphasises the need for support, compassion and trust, and it highlights the need for the family to become involved in the treatment. Had Mrs Hunt done this, she might have learned about these necessary adjuncts to hospital care and might even have been able to practise them.

In the cases we have shown, children have not been involved, but where there are children they obviously suffer a great deal too, because of the fear and uncertainty which pervade the household and which can have a profound effect on the developing personality. It is interesting that a great many alcoholics have themselves been deprived in childhood. The families of alcoholics do need help, if only to provide respite from the stresses and strains that the presence of alcoholism can have on the family. Sometimes, social 'first aid' is also necessary as regards money, food and clothing, because of the dire financial straits that alcoholism brings in its wake. More importantly, it is necessary to give moral encouragement to the family, and in the last resort, if it is going to break up, its members will also need support, advice and guidance to help them deal with this.

references

Rathod, N. 'What is Addiction?' in *Where on Drugs*. Advisory Centre for Education, No date.

World Health Organisation. 'Expert Committee on Addiction – Producing Drugs.' Fifteenth Report. *Tech. Rep. Ser.* 273, 1964.

Glatt, M. M., Pittman, D. J., Gillespie, D. G. and Hills, D. R. *The Drug Scene in Great Britain*. Edward Arnold (Publishers Ltd.). London, 1967.

Munro, A. and McCulloch, W. *Psychiatry for Social Workers*. Pergamon. Oxford, 1969.

Mitchell, A. 'Advice to Parents' in *Where on Drugs*. Advisory Centre for Education, No date.

World Health Organisation. *Technical Report Series* 48. 1952.

Kessel, N. and Grossman, G. 'Suicide in Alcoholics.' *Brit. Med. J.* 2, 1961.

recommended reading

Office of Health Economics. *Drug Addiction*. London, 1967.

Home Office. *The Rehabilitation of Drug Addicts.* H.M.S.O. 1969.
Where on Drugs. See under references above.
Office of Health Economics. *Alcohol Abuse.* London, 1970.
Kessel, N. and Walton, H. *Alcoholism.* Penguin. Harmondsworth, 1967.

8 Social aspects of suicidal behaviour

'Suicide is a problem which confronts all members of the community . . . it is imperative that . . . interested lay bodies like the Samaritans learn the facts about suicidal behaviour in all its forms . . . it is difficult to comprehend the fact that in the world, every year, the equivalent of the population of a city such as Edinburgh or Helsinki kills itself. In addition, in the same period of time the equivalent of the population of London indulges in some form of non-fatal suicidal behaviour.' (McCulloch & Philip, 1972.)

Because the threat of suicide can provoke more anxiety than the threat of murder, it becomes important to allay the associated fears and equally important to correct popular misconceptions.

Although in this chapter we shall deal mainly with non-fatal suicidal behaviour, there is much evidence to suggest that, although the majority of people who kill themselves do so at the first attempt, very many of them will previously have given some indication that the thought of suicide was on their minds. So it becomes important that the reader should learn to be on the lookout for possible warning signs, *particularly in the case of the person suffering from depression.* In Chapter 3 we presented the case of Mr Sheldon who was depressed. We pointed out how the deterioration in his work behaviour was not recognised as being due to his illness, even though his wife had in fact noticed symptoms for some time. Although not referred to specifically in this case study, his wife was able to say that during the period in question, Mr Sheldon had unexpectedly gone to his lawyer and made a will, which he had discussed with her in terms of 'looking after her future'. In addition, his personal papers had been tidied and left in a fairly conspicuous place.

This is a typical kind of warning which the suicidal person frequently gives, and it is behaviour like this for which a relative should be on the alert in the presence of a depressive illness.

A rather different warning was given by Mrs Harris, whose case we discussed in Chapter 5. It will be recalled that her body was discovered by her son who had called to see her one evening. In fact, her son normally called on that particular evening of each week, but had not attached much importance to the fact that, on his previous visit, Mrs Harris had told him not to bother coming next time because she might be out. It never crossed his mind that his elderly mother had not gone out since her bereavement. Here again, in retrospect, there may have been a warning.

'Fortunately, no one is 100% suicidal. Psychologists today realise that even the most ardent death wish is ambivalent. People cut their throats and plead to be saved at the same moment. Suicide notes often illustrate the fatal illogic of the suicidal person, the mixing of crossed-purpose desires: 'Dear Mary, I hate you. Love John.' 'I'm tired. There must be something fine for you. Love Bill.' These simple but pathetic messages are actual suicide notes. Like the iceberg's tip above the surface, they hint at the awesome mass below. When a man is suicidal his perspective freezes. He wants to live, but can see no way. His logic is confused, but he cannot clear his head. He stumbles into death, still grasping for life, even in those last moments when he tries to write down how he feels.' (Schneidman and Mandelkorn, 1967.)

We have indicated that people frequently give warnings of

their suicidal intent, but even when these warnings are heard they are sometimes ignored, because of common misconceptions. The commonest of these misconceptions can be listed as follows:

(1) *When people talk about committing suicide, they rarely do.* This is patently not true.

(2) *There is never any warning before a suicide.* In fact, there are studies which show very clearly that people who have suicidal intent give many clues and warnings.

(3) *People who are suicidal are completely intent on dying.* We have already indicated that this is not so.

(4) *Once a person is suicidal, he is suicidal for ever.* The truth is that, since suicidal behaviour is very commonly associated with a depressive illness and since depressive illnesses get better, the suicidal impulse dies with the remission of the illness. In addition, depression is commonly a 'once in a lifetime' illness.

(5) *Improvement which follows a suicidal crisis, particularly in the case of a depression, means that the risk is over.* This is certainly not the case and it has been estimated that most suicides occur within two to three months after the beginning of improvement and at the time when the individual is sufficiently recovered to put his morbid thoughts and feelings into effect.

The reader may recall from our discussion of depression in Chapter 6 that, when a person is deeply depressed, his actions and his thinking are extremely slowed down and that during this very low ebb he is often unable to act on his suicidal thoughts. We demonstrated in the case of Mr Noble, in that chapter, that he committed suicide at a point when he felt better, when his relatives, observing his improvement, insisted on procuring his discharge, but when in fact, he had just gained sufficient improvement to put into effect the suicidal inclinations he had been pondering for some time.

(6) *Suicide is much more common among the wealthy. (Or alternatively, only poor people kill themselves.)* Such statements are untrue. Suicide is represented at all income levels. We have already indicated that the illness most commonly associated

with suicidal behaviour is depression and, since depressive illness is no respecter of wealth, perhaps this explains the highly 'democratic' nature of suicide.

(7) *Suicide runs through families from generation to generation.* This is not the case, but it must be pointed out that, although suicide adopts an individual pattern, it is often associated with depression and some depressive illnesses can be shown to run in families. It is likely that this is the reason for this misconception.

(8) *People who are suicidal must be mentally ill.* In fact, in studies conducted by one of the present authors (J. W. McC.) it was found that, among a large group of people who had attempted suicide, about a quarter were not psychiatrically ill. Other studies have likewise indicated very clearly that, although the suicidal person is extremely unhappy, he is not necessarily mentally ill.

In essence then, when a person talks of suicide, such talk should not be regarded as an idle threat. Frequently, it is sufficient to allow the person to talk about his feelings and to listen to these sympathetically and this will be enough to prevent an attempt. However, since there is such finality about suicide, no chances should be taken and expert help should be sought. This help is available from many sources such as the *Telephone Samaritans*, general practitioners and social workers. Because of the notion of 'sin' which is often associated with taking one's own life, it is not uncommon for members of the clergy to be called in. There are members of the clergy who know how to handle this kind of situation, but generally speaking we would not recommend this. One reason for saying so is that, as we have shown in Chapters 3 and 4, the depressed person is frequently guilt ridden. In the presence of a representative of the Church (of whatever denomination), who is not highly skilled, there may be an implied judgement and this might only serve to worsen the condition. This may well have historical connotations – as we noted in Chapter 1. We would, however, like to emphasise the sterling work done by the *Telephone Samaritans* – an organisation founded by a member of the clergy and indeed containing among its membership many clergymen. But these are specially trained people, whatever their vocation may be.

Besides seeking skilled help, there is one very important precaution that relatives can take in order to minimise the risk of suicide. Since, as we have pointed out, depressive illness carries a high risk, relatives would be well advised to see to it that the drugs given for this illness are under *their* control and not that of the patient. As we shall point out, suicidal behaviour tends to be an impulsive act and if the means are at hand, they may be used on the spur of the moment.

Taking the steps we have recommended can be difficult, but for the peace of mind of the recipient of the suicidal threat, it is important that he can say, if unhappily his efforts have failed, that he did all he could. There is little doubt that, despite even the most skilled intervention, suicide will still occur in some cases.

It is vital to pay attention to what the person is saying. As we pointed out at the very beginning of this chapter, suicidal behaviour is a vast problem and cuts across class, wealth, colour and creed. It seems anomalous that the public are very willing and able to take action to reduce the number of road accidents, but less so to reduce the number of suicides, when the numbers of people involved in both types of phenomenon are almost the same.

Thus far, we have discussed the risk of suicide, the reactions to suicidal threats and the actions that should be taken by way of intervention. As we indicated early in the chapter, non-fatal suicide occurs from 12 to 20 times more frequently than completed suicide. We propose now to consider some of the factors associated with the latter and its social concommittants.

The social aspects of suicidal behaviour were first discussed in detail by Durkheim in the late nineteenth century, but he was concerned less with individual cases, than with the influence of society on people. Since, as we shall show later, interpersonal relationships and environmental circumstances are important factors in suicidal behaviour, besides considering the individual we must also discuss the environment. There is an excellent account of the varied social and philosophical attitudes towards suicide in a book by Dublin entitled *Suicide: A Sociological and Statistical Study*. This author has postulated that for the Stoic, suicide could be seen as an honourable act, whereas for the Jew and the Christian it has always been sinful and blasphemous (See Chapter 1.). Current lay opinion still has many of its roots in this latter attitude, with the result that suicidal behaviour tends to be seen as a result of weakness of character. As we pointed out earlier, the completed suicide tends to be regarded posthumously as having been of unsound mind. People who try to kill themselves, but who survive, are seen either as having 'failed' or as 'having made a gesture'. Over the years, the idea has grown that attempted suicide is failed suicide, but in fact, attempted suicide is neither a *diagnosis* nor a *description of behaviour*. It is an interpretation of behaviour which is extremely difficult to quantify.

After Durkheim's turn-of-the-century work on the social aspects of suicidal behaviour, there was a considerable lapse in the pursuit of this aspect. One of the main reasons for this delay was the fact that many of the early studies emanated from mental hospitals and were therefore sponsored almost exclusively by psychiatrists. This may also have accounted for the other assumption, that attempted and completed suicides were alike in all aspects save one – the fact of survival. This assumption probably arose because, of suicidal individuals who survived, only those who were the most seriously disturbed psychiatrically were admitted to mental hospital. In these circumstances, it is easy to understand why such a highly-selected hospital population would closely resemble the group of people whose suicidal actions had resulted in death.

The law also played its part in establishing the apparent extent and nature of the problem of suicidal behaviour, for, until recently, it was a criminal offence to attempt suicide in many countries, including England and Wales (but not Scotland). This, undoubtedly, led to a good deal of 'covering up' by relatives and family doctors. Yet another misleading aspect, as we have pointed out, was the mistaken belief that suicidal behaviour *must* be an evidence of mental illness. It is likely that, because of this, many attempts were hushed up so as to prevent a loved one being 'shut up' in an asylum. This was often because of the stigma attached to mental illness, but in many cases because the people who attempted suicide did not appear to be mentally ill after physical recovery.

One very important factor which still further delayed the acquisition of knowledge in this field was the mistaken idea that there was a direct association between the quantity of drugs taken in a suicide attempt and the seriousness of the act. Partly due to lack of knowledge about drugs, it is possible for a person who is hell-bent on killing himself to swallow six tablets because the instructions on the bottle say, 'Do not exceed two tablets at any one time,' only to find that there has been no ill-effect because the manufacturer has been rightly over-cautious. Conversely, a reckless individual may swallow an enormous amount of poison because of a mistaken assumption that it is relatively harmless.

In more recent years there have been many studies which have been concerned with the socio-psychological aspects of suicidal behaviour and these have revealed some of the associated indicators which we shall now discuss.

the influence of emotion

It is important to consider the social implications of the part played by emotions such as jealousy, anger, spite and hate in relation to suicidal behaviour. These are often difficult to separate from each other and it is not easy to establish a clear relationship between any one emotion and suicidal behaviour, since anger, hate and spite can, for example, all spring from jealousy. It has been suggested that, when a person indulges in non-fatal suicidal behaviour based on all or any of the emotions described above, this may be because he is so basically insecure that he cannot satisfactorily express the emotion either outwardly or inwardly. Some studies have shown that in cases of attempted suicide among children and young people, there is a high incidence of jealousy and anger. In such cases, the attempt may often be seen as one of rebellion against a parent or other close figure, whose behaviour has been perceived as unduly restrictive. The underlying postulation could be that the intent was to frighten the person concerned into a change of attitude or behaviour. The case we now present indicates this.

case 1 Miss Cartwright

Miss Cartwright was a sixteen-year-old schoolgirl with a hysterical personality. (See Chapter 6). She had been 'stood up'. This occurrence, as we showed, is not uncommon with this type of personality. An hour after the appointed meeting time, she went to a telephone box immediately outside the gates of the casualty hospital and telephoned her boy friend's home. She said to his mother – 'If you can't make John come to see me now, I will take an overdose of aspirin'. John did not turn up. Miss Cartwright took ten aspirins and walked into the casualty department.

An important point we wish to make here is that had John 'come running' to her, either in the face of the threat or as a reaction to the overdose, Miss Cartwright's manipulative behaviour would have been reinforced. In other words, she would have found a way of keeping John and others 'on a string.'

Faced with a situation like this, the 'Johns' of this world would be well advised to take thought and, if possible, to seek expert advice for the following reasons: firstly, because they may need considerable reassurance to relieve their own feelings of anxiety and guilt about the incident, since they may well feel at least partly responsible: and secondly, to be sure that their interpretation of the act, in relation to the person who carried it out, was the correct one. It is just possible that the person concerned may *not* have been behaving in a purely manipulative fashion but could, for example, be depressed and impulsive.

interpersonal relationship problems

The case of Miss Cartwright of course involved interpersonal relationships, but demonstrated more clearly the anger and spite aspect of behaviour involving self-injury. Now we shall consider interpersonal relationships of a much deeper nature.

disturbed childhood experiences: There are two main aspects of disturbances in childhood caused by loss of a parent by death or desertion. In the case of death, psychoanalytic theory postulates that there is an association between such an experience and a tendency to depressive illness later in life. We have already shown the relationship between depression and suicidal behaviour and it has been theorised that, when the loss of a loved one occurs in the middle years of childhood, or in late adolescence, the child would hate the 'love object' who, he felt, had betrayed and deserted him. Not surprisingly, feeling so angry may bring on guilt feelings (also associated with depression) and this could result in self-punishment. Alternatively, it has been suggested that the loss of a parent in early childhood, by death, separation, or withdrawal through disturbed parental relationship, may have a powerful bearing on the genesis of abnormalities of personality. Among people who attempt suicide, probably as many as a quarter carry a diagnosis of personality disorder. Further, amongst people who make more than one suicidal attempt, the proportion who can be diagnosed as personality-disordered almost doubles. In Chapters 6 and 7 we discussed the impulsivity found as a feature in some of the personality disorders and also the relationship between abnormalities of personality and a tendency to develop addictions. Since people who are addicted to drugs or alcohol frequently indulge in suicidal behaviour (often with fatal consequences), and since we have said that suicidal behaviour is in itself an impulsive act, this group of people must be particularly vulnerable. Studies of attempted suicide have shown that people with personality abnormalities and their families often show very severe psychosocial pathology in the form of alcoholism, neglect, brutality, delinquency and crime. It has been noted that, generally, these were people who grew up in an environment in which impulses were not merely fantasied but *real*, because they were habitually acted out.

'Petty crime, prostitution and many other forms of degradation are witnessed as part of daily living. These people have been reared in a world where actions speak louder than words; where impulsiveness is dominant; and where people live from day to day with weak ties to a meaningful past and little investment in the future. To this way of life it is nearly certain that we must now add "suicidal behaviour." ' (McCulloch, 1971.)

Other authors have consistently pointed to the importance of parent-child relationships in the study of suicidal behaviour and, from the many works on the emotional development of children, there is strong evidence to suggest that disturbances in child-parent relationships have a profound and often lasting deleterious effect on the child. A case which typifies the relationship between the factors quoted above and suicidal behaviour was that of Mr Wilcox (Chapter 6). We will not present further examples of the depressive element in this section since these have already been well described in Chapters 3 and 4.

marital disharmony: It is difficult to assess the true extent of marital and love problems in relation to attempted suicide, because of the varying methods of reporting adopted by investigators. Some report the incidence of disharmony as a proportion of the entire group under study, some as a proportion of only the married people, and some have grouped all amatory disturbances together with marital disharmony, so that the picture is somewhat obscured. Nevertheless, the fact is that very many investigators have reported such disturbances either as contributing factors leading eventually to suicidal behaviour, or as actual precipitants. Not surprisingly, disturbances of this nature are more likely to occur in the background of individuals with personality abnormalities than in those with other forms of psychiatric diagnosis or those with no discernible psychiatric illness. It is very obvious that the individual with a personality disorder finds it hard to make deep and lasting relationships and this fact infiltrates his whole life situation. Nevertheless, such people marry impulsively, have children impulsively, and often leave home impulsively. This pattern of behaviour was well exemplified in the case of Mr Wilcox.

We shall now illustrate a case of self-injury where there was no notable abnormality of personality:

case 2 Mrs Watson

Mrs Watson, aged 22, married with four small children was

admitted to hospital following a suicidal attempt, having taken a whole bottle of sleeping tablets which had been prescribed by her general practitioner. She met her husband when she was 18 and married him after a whirlwind courtship. At the time of the marriage she was a perfectly normal young woman with a very ordinary background, and a good work and health record. During courtship, her husband had idolised her and generally put her on a pedestal. The attention he paid was indeed flattering to her and it was this that promoted the early marriage. She had noticed that he was a little jealous of other men who spoke to her, but she was also flattered by this.

She fell pregnant very quickly after marriage and realised, almost as quickly, that her husband's jealousy went much deeper than she had thought. Every time she had been out, she would be questioned on her return about the men she might have spoken to, or sat beside on buses. To shorten the story somewhat, she had a baby every year up to the point of her admission to hospital and her husband's jealousy increased as time went on, until the point was reached when he began to examine her underclothing when he came home at night, in an effort to find out if she had been having sexual intercourse.

It can readily be understood what extreme anguish and stress her husband's behaviour caused. This, together with the presence of four very small children, and the possibility of more to come, was too much for Mrs Watson. She could see no way out of the predicament and took an overdose. There was no evidence of any psychiatric abnormality in this young woman's case. On discharge she instituted divorce proceedings which, when effected, returned her to her previous normal self.

This case typifies not only a fractured marital relationship but also demonstrates that stress is not solely the province of psychiatry and that attempted suicide can occur in people who are not mentally ill. There is little doubt that, given a superabundance of stress, any of us may crack. Another interesting feature of this case is the pathological jealousy of the husband. One might imagine that this should have been obvious to Mrs Watson, but so intent was he on winning her and keeping her that she failed at the time to spot the more sinister aspect of his attentions. Interestingly, *jealous husbands* seem to believe that, by keeping their wives pregnant, they will be unattractive to other men and this was undoubtedly true of Mr Watson. The tragedy of this case was that Mrs Watson had to resort to such dangerous behaviour in order to escape from her predicament. There must have been many people around her who knew what was going on, but who did not want to 'interfere.'

We have used a rather extreme illustration, but there are many similar instances when dejection, as a result of a spouse's or lover's conduct, can result in suicidal behaviour. Disturbances of interpersonal relationships clearly cause unhappiness and even depression. This being so, when people fall out, the mood of the moment frequently takes control and in some cases, unfortunately, impulsivity and anguish combined can lead to suicidal behaviour.

other social factors
financial problems: In this area there are two distinct aspects of difficulties with money. The first is a chronic state of poverty, and the second is a specific precipitating agent. The following two short cases illustrate each of these aspects.

case 3 Mr Hewitt
Mr Hewitt was aged 45, married with 5 children. He had had a lifelong poor employment record and a history of debts. Indeed, he had gone through life in Micawber-like fashion and survived by dint of paying one account at the expense of all others. He was well known to many social work agencies and charitable funds, whose help he frequently sought, but whose doors had largely been closed because of the frequency of his visits.

After waiting for many years, he and his family were allocated a council house. He immediately went out and bought a vast amount of furniture on hire purchase which was subsequently re-possessed. It was this event that appeared to precipitate the attempt at suicide by slashing his wrists whilst under the influence of drink. Mr Hewitt's early life had been one of impoverishment, disorganisation and parental rejection and it was interesting to find that the threatened rejection by his wife in the face of his failure to

support the family, also added to his feelings of hopelessness.
case 4 Mr Rumbold
Mr Rumbold was a fifty-year-old company executive, married with two teenage children. His company had been taken over by a larger concern and he became redundant. The Rumbold family had always lived to the fullest extent of their income and had little or no reserves to fall back on. It was a great shock to become unemployed and to be without regular income other than social security benefit. His feelings of despair about this were compounded as time went on and he was totally unable to find a post that he thought was commensurate with his abilities. He became increasingly sensitive about meeting his old friends and acquaintances. Eventually he developed recognisable clinical depression. His wife became alarmed at the number of times he talked about his failure and how useful it would be to his family if he were to die so that they could have the benefit from his substantial life insurance policies. She persuaded him to visit his G.P. who prescribed anti-depressant drugs which, unfortunately, Mr Rumbold took charge of. One evening, whilst the family was out and were not expected back until very late, he took a massive overdose. Fortunately for him, the family returned very much earlier than expected, found him in a comatose state and had him rushed to hospital where he recovered physically.

He was subsequently transferred to a psychiatric hospital and after successful treatment was discharged with follow-up by a social worker. Between them, they found a means to secure appropriate employment and gradually he regained his confidence and self-esteem.

In Mr Hewitt's case we can see once again the effects of an adverse early environment, characterised classically by lack of insight and foresight, by impulsivity and by poor interpersonal relationships. Handling such a case is difficult because of these factors. People like Mr Hewitt, impulsive as always, very frequently opt out of treatment situations in a precipitate fashion and often, because of their lack of foresight and insight, believe that they can survive without help. Mr Rumbold's case, whilst demonstrating many of the features with which the reader will now be familiar, also produced a rather interesting example of the importance of self-esteem. In Chapters 3 and 4, we indicated that one of the classical symptoms of depressive illness was the loss of self-esteem. Normally, this comes in the wake of the illness, but in Mr Rumbold's case it preceded it and was obviously the result of losing his job. It is more than likely that the development of his depression was accelerated by this. A similar process was also evidenced in the case of Mr Sheldon (Chapter 3) and it need not be stressed how important it is to help to boost the self-esteem of people in Mr Rumbold's position.

problems of employment: Basically there are two types of unemployed people: those who are temporarily out of work and are anxious to resume, and those to whom unemployment can be seen almost as a way of life. Because of the close association between unemployment and finance, we do not propose to present any new cases in this section, since the two previous cases cover both these aspects. It must be remembered however that in this country today, where social security has reached a fairly advanced stage, it is sometimes more advantageous financially to be unemployed than to work, and it follows that within the chronic-unemployed sphere one often finds the Mr Hewitts of this world. On the other hand, people who are psychologically very normal may become quite depressed because of their lack of activity and/or guilt feelings associated with the drawing of benefits when they are *able* to work, but no employment offers itself.

criminality: In discussing personality abnormalities we pointed out the increased likelihood of the presence of criminal behaviour and we have shown that people with such abnormalities are also liable to attempt suicide. However, crime can be a causative factor in suicidal behaviour whether or not there has been a previous background of delinquency. Not infrequently, a fear of prosecution or of imminent detection can be the actual precipitant, as is shown in the case of Mrs Sholto.

case 5 Mrs Sholto
Mrs Sholto was a fifty-five year old widow, with one son living abroad who worked as an executive with an oil com-

pany. Mrs Sholto was the treasurer of a local ladies' organisation and collected her members' subscriptions for the annual outing to the coast. Her son, who was very considerate towards his mother, normally sent her money each month. One month, being short of cash, but expecting his fairly substantial cheque, she borrowed the guild monies. Unfortunately, when the outing was due and she had to pay for the coach and the meal that had been booked, she could not do so, nor could she bring herself to admit her defalcation. Rather than face up to things, she tried to gas herself. Fortunately, a neighbour smelled the gas and she was rescued in time.

Here we have a case of another non-sick person being so much under stress and without helpful resources that she succumbed to intolerable pressure. Like Mr Rumbold, her whole reputation was at stake, and in her mind, that of her son's also. Once again, we can see impulsiveness in her act, then a threat to self-esteem and a resort to the only method which was available to her – the gas oven.

isolation: In Chapter 4 we drew attention to various illnesses which caused people to withdraw from their normal social circle. In the case of the depressive patient, we have already discussed this in relation to his suicidal behaviour and so under the present heading we shall present the case of an old lady who was psychologically sound, so far as is known, but who was very lonely.

case 6 Mrs Hargreaves

Mrs Hargreaves was an eighty-three year old widow with her only child living abroad. She was a friendly old soul who regarded old age philosophically. This was probably due to the satisfactory life that she had led. Although friendly, she was not pushing and derived satisfaction from her independence. She had been developing arthritis for many years and became progressively less able to get around. In her case, her independent outlook probably operated against her because, as she became more immobile and in need of help, her independence was honoured by her near neighbours. Not being able to get out and about, her friendliness had no outlet and she was loth to ask for help because she did not want to be a burden on anyone. At the point at which she felt that this was imminent, she gassed herself and it was several days before she was found.

There are two points worthy of note in this case. Firstly, for old people, a frequent method of suicide is by coal gas poisoning, and this not infrequently causes problems of assessment where recovery occurs. Sometimes, when old ladies are admitted to hospital suffering from coal gas poisoning, they say that they were making tea and that the kettle must have boiled over and put out the gas. Because doctors are in the main charitable people, statements about such accidents are often believed, or at least it seems expedient to believe them, with the result that no further investigation of the patient's circumstances takes place. However, studies have shown that when statements like this are made, it must be remarkable how often tea has been made in the oven. By being charitable, the circumstances which led to the suicide attempt are frequently left uninvestigated and therefore unchanged. The second point, which is, fortunately, now receiving much more attention from local authorities and other organisations, is the need for neighbours and others to notice when an old person is not pursuing her usual activities or when milk bottles remain on a doorstep for several days, or any other change in normal activity.

alcohol: The problem of alcohol abuse has been dealt with at some length in Chapter 7 and we have already given a case illustration – that of Mr Hunt. In the study of one of the present authors (J. W. McC.) referred to earlier, it was found that half of the men and a quarter of the women were either intoxicated, or had been drinking up to the time of the suicidal attempt. The following case, we hope, will help to distinguish the use of alcohol as a *facilitator* from alcohol as the basic *problem*.

case 7 Mr Bolton
Mr Bolton, aged 43, a single man, suffered from multiple sclerosis – a disease which is often accompanied by lability of emotions. As the illness progressed and he became more and more dependent on his elderly mother he decided in quite a calculated way that, because of this and because the

future held little for him anyway, he would do away with himself. To this end, he collected his daily drugs by pretending to take them, until he considered he had sufficient to carry out the act. However, when it came to the point, he could not deliberately 'end it all'.

Being fairly comfortably off and because he did all his entertaining in his bedroom, there were always drinks in his bedside cabinet. Normally a modest drinker, he drank about half a bottle of whisky and then took the tablets. However, because of his inebriated state and his marked shakiness many of the tablets were strewn over the floor beyond his reach. This undoubtedly saved his life, since it was not likely that he would have been disturbed before morning.

Although the cases which we have discussed in this chapter are not all of young people, there does appear to be an age factor in suicidal behaviour, particularly for women. For men, the rates between the ages of 20 and 64 are fairly constant, with teenagers showing about half the rates for adults. For women, however, the peak rates are to be found between 18 and 24, with the teenage rates being the highest of all.

There is no identifiable profile of a suicidal type, but according to McCulloch and Philip (1972) there are some traits which are associated with such behaviour. For men, 'this type of person is a "loner" who pays little heed to the needs and expectations of society, experiences little desire for close personal contacts, is emotionally volatile, and is prone to be extra-punitive. Such a synthesis has a striking resemblance to . . . the concept of the psychopath . . .' The female type which emerges is 'that of a woman who is emotionally labile and impulsive, complains about lack of energy, is dissatisfied with life, and tends to be apprehensive and guilt-prone. Despite producing a wealth of symptomatology, she tends to be diagnosed as a disordered personality and has a poor social prognosis.'

We have tried to show that social events are not the only factors which are associated with attempted suicide. Sometimes the factors involved are the result of underlying physical illness or disability, mental illness, mental subnormality, or personality abnormality. The stresses involved are frequently multiple and often of long standing. We hope the reader will have observed that the presence of interacting social factors often tells us more about the patient's personality than about the motivation for the act itself. It would be dangerous to assume that there is necessarily a causal relationship between the social and the other factors we have described, which are frequently referred to as precipitants, and suicidal behaviour.

Although patients may be prepared to say 'I did it because . . .' the interpretation of the motive and the intent may still have to be inferred. It is easier for a person, under so much stress that he wants to die, to produce a motive from a real life situation, than to have to admit that he did not really know why he behaved as he did. As we have repeatedly pointed out, attempted suicide is mostly impulsive and many of the people who indulge in this behaviour may never have formulated their intention or have thought about the outcome of their act.

references

McCulloch, J. W. and Philip, A. E. *Suicidal Behaviour*. Pergamon. Oxford, 1972.

Schneidman, E. A. and Mandelkorn, P. *How to Prevent Suicide*. Public Affairs Pamphlet, No. 46, Public Affairs Committee Inc. New York, 1967.

McCulloch, J. W. 'Social Aspects of Acute Barbiturate Poisoning' in *Acute Barbiturate Poisoning*. Ed. Matthew, H. Excerpta Medica Monograph. Amsterdam, 1971.

recommended reading

McCulloch and Philip. See references above.

Dublin, L. I. *Suicide: a sociological and statistical study*. Ronald Press, New York, 1963.

Clarke, A. D. B. and Clarke, A. M. 'Some Recent Advances in the Study of Early Deprivation.' *J. Child Psychol. and Psychiat. I.* 26–36, 1962.

Stengel, E. *Suicide and Attempted Suicide*. Penguin. Harmondsworth, 1964.

9 Mental subnormality...
mental handicap

So far in this book we have been discussing the social problems associated with *psychiatric illness*. We now turn to a consideration of some of the social problems associated with *mental subnormality*. Although, as will be seen in Chapter 10, the law classifies mental subnormality under the heading of mental disorder, it is necessary both from a clinical and a social point of view to distinguish the two conditions. Mental illness and mental subnormallty can exist, however, in the same person, as we shall show later.

Mental subnormality, or mental deficiency as it used to be called, is very much a relative concept. It is often wrongly assumed that the degree of subnormality can be assessed purely in terms of intellectual capacity. Whilst this is obviously important, as will be seen later, it is essential to have equal regard for the *social functioning* of the individual and for the environment in which he lives. In this chapter we shall be particularly concerned to deal with some of the problems that the mentally subnormal present to those who have to care for them – notably their families.

In Chapter 1 passing reference was made to the history of the care of the subnormal. This will now be elaborated upon briefly. Before the nineteenth century, the mentally subnormal had either been abused or worshipped, according to the pressures and demands of the society in which they lived. Christianity had always included in its teaching some degree of compassion, but with the gradual development of the 'puritan' ethic, social performance, or the lack of it, tended to bring about a degree of condemnation.

In small rural communities those mentally handicapped persons who survived at least had some place; at a time when few people could read and write and before the introduction of machinery demanded skill and training for employment, the 'village idiot' could be accepted as part of his community.

From the middle of the nineteenth century onwards, there was a growing fear of national degeneracy, encouraged by the work of early eugenicists such as Francis Galton. Incredible though it may seem to us today, in 1910 the members of the National Association for the Care of the Feeble Minded were asking every Parliamentary candidate to support measures that 'tend to discourage parenthood on the part of the feeble minded and other degenerate types'. The permanent segregation of the mentally handicapped, alongside (it must be added) the mentally ill, from the rest of society became the only, and highly Draconian answer. Such small attempts as there had been at education seemed to have given way to custody. The mentally handicapped and their care passed from the early pioneers of remedial education to the medical profession, the people who understood genetics, and who were thought able to take on unsupportable behaviour which, in the small communities of early days, had been accepted without undue concern.

However, public interest continued and there were some forward-looking efforts to provide education for the more mildly mentally handicapped; the rest were still consigned to the workhouses, lunatic asylums, and indeed the gaols. Two Royal Commissions had reported at the end of the nineteenth century and had recommended the introduction of special provision for the mentally defective. Many of these recommendations were written into the Mental Deficiency Act of 1913. This Act created four categories of mental defectives:

idiots and imbeciles; the *feeble minded*; and *moral imbeciles*. The Act, useful as it was in some ways, bearing in mind the climate of the times, unfortunately laid more emphasis on segregation and laid down the standards of care (except for some minor modifications in the late 1920s) that were to govern procedure until the Mental Health Act of 1959.

Despite recommendations for more community interest in the mentally handicapped during the 1920s, they remained mainly in institutions, with little attempt being made to apply the remedial measures advocated by the nineteenth century pioneers. As late as 1927, even the fairly progressive Board of Control could say of the mentally deficient that they were 'exposed to temptations that they have no power to resist, a misery to themselves and a source of danger to their neighbours.'

Until fairly recently, one of the most crucial problems facing the mentally subnormal was the lack of concern (with a few noticeable exceptions) of professions other than medicine and nursing. In recent years, however, the growing interest in problems of child development, in aspects of community care, and in the encouragement of self-help groups for a variety of handicaps have had a marked impact on the development of care for the subnormal.

The intention in the 1959 Mental Health Act to replace institutional provision by care in the community was laudable, but a recent Government report entitled 'Better Services for the Mentally Handicapped' (1971) indicates that there is an enormous shortfall in the number of places that will be needed in hostels, half-way houses, sheltered accommodation, workshops and elsewhere if the intentions contained in the Act are ever to become realities.

definitions

From a historical point of view it is interesting to note how we have passed through phases of speaking about *idiocy*, to *defectiveness*, and *feeble-mindedness* to *subnormality*, and now more generically, to speak of *mental handicap* or *retardation*. As a generalisation, it can be said that psychiatrists in the field of subnormality still tend to prefer to speak of mental deficiency whilst social workers and psychologists prefer the terms mental handicap or retardation.

Earlier, we cautioned about the dangers of defining mental handicap purely in terms of intellectual capacity as expressed in an intelligence quotient (I.Q.). However, in giving some indication of the range of handicap the I.Q. provides us with an approximate measure. It is usually suggested that there are four major degrees of mental handicap:

(1) Mild mental handicap (subnormality or retardation). I.Q. range 52–67.

(2) Moderate mental handicap. Persons so handicapped can learn to care for themselves. Adults so handicapped need, as a rule, to work in sheltered employment. I.Q. range 36–51.

(3) Severe mental handicap. Persons so handicapped are often physically handicapped as well. I.Q. range 20–35.

(4) Profound mental handicap. Persons so handicapped are quite unable to care for themselves and normally require hospital care. I.Q. less than 20.

It should be emphasised at this point that the foregoing are clinical and not legal classifications. The Mental Health Act 1959 recognises only two forms of mental handicap: (a) *subnormality* and (b) *severe subnormality*.

As we shall show a little later in this chapter, the environment of the mentally handicapped individual and the attitudes of those who care for him either in an institution or in his own home will affect profoundly his performance and capacities. Unhappily, although there is undoubtedly increasing concern about the needs of the mentally handicapped, ours is an age in which increasing emphasis is placed upon achievement and the acquiring of technical and other skills, and so the subnormal individual in our community becomes increasingly vulnerable.

the size of the problem

It is very difficult to give an accurate indication of the numbers of subnormal people in the population, particularly those who are mildly subnormal, since for reasons which we will give later, they may never come to official attention. It is much easier to give numbers of severely mentally handicapped people, since in general their problems are more clearly discernable, particularly if they are physically handicapped as well. As a rough guide we can say that (a) there are some 51,000 children in schools for the educationally subnormal and a further 11,000 on waiting lists. (b) There are some 60,000 persons in hospitals for the subnormal. (c) There are about 96,000 mentally subnormal people known to local authorities for one reason or another. In all, there are between two and three severely mentally handicapped people in every thousand members of the population. An important point to be made here is that, with advances in medical care and a continuing decrease in infant mortality, the numbers of severely mentally handicapped children who survive will probably increase, though in time, genetic counselling and improved antenatal diagnosis of conditions causing mental handicap may bring about a reduction in the size of the problem.

the recognition of the problem

There are a number of ways in which subnormality in children may come to attention. For example, children with certain specific congenital conditions (such as chromosome abnormalities) are reported to the office of the Registrar General. In addition, babies in whom there are complications during pregnancy and at birth may be placed on an 'At Risk' register of the local health department. This can also be done at any subsequent point before school entry is reached if there are signs of delayed or abnormal development. Other opportunities for recognition and, incidentally, counselling are available through special clinics within the Maternity and Child Welfare Service or at the out-patient departments of subnormality or general hospitals. There is a requirement that all newly-born children should be visited by a Health Visitor during their first two years of life and during these visits it may be possible to observe any obvious signs of mental subnormality. This is not to say that mental subnormality can necessarily be recognised readily, as we shall shortly show in a case presentation. Recognition of subnormality is also part of the educational system and handicapped children may eventually be picked out when they start to fail at any point in their scholastic careers. If such cases arise and there are other children in the family, the younger pre-school members can also be investigated.

In most instances, the more severe forms of mental subnormality are recognised at some stage in childhood or early adolescence. However, some children may escape the screening process and their subnormality only becomes apparent in adult life. Such cases may be picked up by agencies like the Department of Employment and Social Security, Probation Officers, the Police, Social Workers in General Hospitals, General Practitioners and Personnel Officers in factories.

causal factors

At the beginning of this chapter we mentioned that *mental subnormality* was frequently confused in the public mind with *mental illness*. In general terms it can be said that the mentally ill person begins life with normal intellectual endowments but, for a variety of reasons, becomes ill and thus deviates from normality, whereas the mentally subnormal person never had the endowment of 'normality', or lost it in infancy. This point is shown very clearly in one of the early descriptive terms used for mental subnormality – *amentia* – which literally means 'lack of mind.'

There are nearly three hundred known causes of mental handicap but it is only possible to define an exact cause in about 35 per cent of cases. Some of the chief causes are summarised as follows:

(1) *Mental handicap due to disease in the parent* such as Rubella (German Measles). In these cases there is a one-in-ten chance of a mentally handicapped child being born if the mother develops the disease early in pregnancy. Nowadays, young girls are often offered vaccination against the disease so that this risk can be avoided.

Diseases in early childhood such as Meningitis or Encephalitis can also sometimes lead to mental subnormality as a result of brain-damage.

(2) *Radiation hazards:* It has been shown that pregnant women exposed to the effects of radiation can produce sub-

normal children. However, stringent precautions are normally taken to avoid this hazard, so that abdominal X-rays are avoided as much as possible during pregnancy.

(3) *Drugs:* There is some evidence to suggest that if a pregnant woman has abused certain drugs, such as L.S.D. (see Chapter 7) there is a risk of her giving birth to a mentally subnormal baby. Certain therapeutic drugs can also cause damage – Thalidomide being the most notorious – but nowadays stringent precautions are taken over the use of these.

(4) *Brain damage:* In Chapter V we made some reference to disease caused by damage to the brain. Such damage can be caused to a child either *before, during,* or *after* birth. One condition that can result from brain abnormality is Hydrocephalus. This, however, can often be remedied by surgical intervention.

(5) *Mental handicap due to chromosome abnormalities:* The best known of these is *Mongolism* or Down's Syndrome (after Langdon-Down who first identified it). It has been calculated that for every 700 births, there is likely to be one mongol. However, the incidence varies from one in 2,300 births, if the mother is 20 years old, to one in 54 if the mother is 45 years old or more. It is now possible to detect this abnormality before birth by a remarkable procedure in which a quantity of the fluid surrounding the foetus is drawn off and subjected to laboratory analysis. It has been suggested that if this service were to become more generally available, all mothers with an affected pregnancy could be offered a termination of the pregnancy and also be informed of the possible risks of further mongol births.

(6) *Other 'inborn' causes:* One of the best known of these is *Phenylketonuria*. This is found in about one child in 20,000. Children with this condition are unable to cope with the Phenylalanine content of normal diets. If a special diet is observed, normal development occurs. If the diet is not observed, severe mental handicap ensues. These days, all newly-born infants are given a simple routine test for this. *Cretinism* (due to thyroid deficiency) used to be quite a common cause of mental subnormality. Fortunately it is now rare, since

the deficiency in the thyroid gland can be rectified by the giving of thyroid hormone.

It must be remembered that where there is mild subnormality this can be exacerbated by things such as a lack of social and intellectual stimulation, malnutrition and poor ante- and post-natal care.

problems associated with mental subnormality

Because of the intractable nature of mental subnormality and the need for long-term care we propose to deal mainly with the caring aspect and the impact of mental subnormality on the family in the cases which follow:

case 1 John

John, aged 11, was an only child of a well-to-do family. He was a bright-looking and rather handsome boy. He was admitted to a children's home after his father and mother separated. One of the noticeable features on admission was a rather 'stunned' look which was thought to be a kind of shocked effect associated with having to leave home. It soon became obvious that there was a certain 'vacant' quality to this look which as time went by appeared in the face of any little perplexity. Before admission he had attended one of the better private schools in the country, but after admission he attended a local comprehensive school. It soon became evident that his school work was far below the level of his peers ... Again, this was put down to the trauma of separation, but later intellectual testing showed him to have an I.Q. (Intelligence Quotient) in the region of 60 plus — which is well within the midly subnormal range. As a result of these tests special education was arranged and there was a marked change in his happiness and functioning.

From what could be gathered about the parents — the father never came to see him and the mother only very rarely — they seemed to have been a fairly happy couple until John started primary school. Father was apparently a rather obsessional personality — a perfectionist. When it became apparent that *his* son did not appear to be getting on as well as the other children, he applied more than a little pressure on the boy and gave him extra tuition to help him to catch up. This brought many tears from the boy and recriminations from the father. Mother's reaction to this was to blame her husband's pressure for the boy's seeming lack of progress. This caused many violent arguments which must only have added to the boy's distress. John was removed from the local school – in his father's eyes he had become 'incompetent' and a series of private schools followed. Ultimately, because of the friction at home, and mother's increasing insistence that father's intervention was the cause of John's lack of progress, it was decided, when he was nine years old, to put him into a boarding school. John's separation from his parents did nothing to reduce the marital disharmony – in fact it increased it, with mother blaming her husband for the loss of her son.

Within a year of John's leaving home, father had gone off with another woman. For a time, John's mother was able to remain in the family home and to keep a certain amount of contact with him. Ultimately, father went abroad and the alimony stopped. John's mother, never having worked, was completely unable to face up to her new situation and returned to her parental home. It was suspected that John's maternal grandparents were instrumental in causing the final separation. Although they were wealthy and prepared to support his mother, they refused to pay John's school fees. Shortly afterwards, mother had a mental illness of the anxiety-depressive type. The grandparents refused to look after John during mother's sojourn in hospital and had him admitted to the children's home.

This case shows vividly the father's inability to accept John's handicap and the effects of his subsequent unrealistic expectations on the boy. The reader will have noticed how he apportioned blame to mother's coddling, school incompetence and even marital disharmony. It is noticeable also that he subsequently denied his parental responsibilities altogether, but even in doing this the blame was apportioned to the marital disharmony. It was as though he *had* to cut himself off from involvement. It is interesting also that John's maternal grandparents, although behaving superficially differently, reacted in basically the same way. Mother, too, was seen to be unable to accept John's limitations and she found a way to project the blame. In her case, however, this was at a more obvious price and although one cannot be certain (because of her non-contact), it is likely that this price was a depressive illness, probably caused by the underlying guilt that she felt.

case 2 Jane

Jane, aged 19 years, was the daughter of middle-aged parents and an only child. Father was a security officer for a large industrial concern. Because of the large size of her head, it was obvious right from birth that Jane was *hydrocephalic*. In addition, she was severely physically disabled and required constant nursing care and attention. Her parents decided very early on that they would not place Jane in hospital care because they loved her and felt they should care for her by themselves. In the event, this was comparatively easy when Jane was very small and her parents comparatively young. As she grew older, the burden became more and more heavy.

Jane's parents found that opportunities for getting out and about became less and less possible and that friends and neighbours visited less frequently and gave the impression that it was not because they didn't want to help Jane's parents, but because they appeared to be afraid of Jane.

When Jane was 21 years old, her mother developed angina. This made for difficulties in caring for Jane's physical needs and father had frequently to take time off work to help out.

Eventually father, went to see the welfare officer at his work because he felt that the situation had reached such a crisis point that he would have to give up work. The welfare officer put him into contact with the local authority social services department who were able to arrange for the services of a Home Help. They also arranged temporary hospital admission for Jane for regular short periods, so that her parents could have holidays. In addition, a social worker was assigned to the case, so that she could reassure Jane's parents that longer-term care could be arranged when they were no longer able to cope by themselves.

Given this help, Jane's parents were able to relax somewhat. With the new arrangements and support, they looked forward to being able to care for their daughter.

This case highlights some of the difficulties facing parents who choose to rear and care for their mentally and physically handicapped children at home. Quite apart from the physical demands on such parents, there is the accompanying sense of isolation which is often associated with prolonged grief. In addition, as this case illustrates, parents are often much preoccupied with what will happen to their child in the event of their death; some reassurance is necessary in order to help them to cope with these feelings. The reader will have noticed that help *is* available, both in terms of physical and emotional support, for parents in this kind of situation.

case 3 Mary

Mary, aged 13 years, was the youngest of three children. She was mentally retarded as the result of her mother having contracted German Measles during the second month of her pregnancy. In addition to her moderate degree of mental handicap, Mary presented problems of behaviour such as aggressive outbursts and excessive demands for attention.

As a baby, although her mother was worried as to what the future would hold (being aware of the possible effects of German Measles), Mary posed no overt problems. Nevertheless, her mother paid a great amount of attention to her – often at the expense of the two older children.

By the age of three, Mary began to show evidence of demanding and aggressive behaviour and this worsened as she approached early adolescence. More and more, Mary's older sisters were left to their own devices. Indeed, their mother was almost pleased when they got out from 'under her feet'. This apparent lack of maternal approach resulted in both the older children appearing before the Court for shop-lifting – an offence which they had committed in concert.

As a result of these first offences, a Probation Officer called at the home to prepare a report for the Magistrates and it was at this point that the stressful home situation was uncovered. He found that Mary's father appeared to have opted out. He was quite unable to tolerate the home situation. Thinking that Mary's behaviour was controllable, he blamed his wife for what he regarded as her bad handling, spending much of his time in the 'local'. This also meant that he had little time to spend with his two older children.

Because of the knowledge brought to the Court by the

Probation Officer, Mary's older sisters were placed under supervision and arrangements were made, with the parents' agreement, for Mary to be admitted to a Residential Special School.

This case illustrates the extent to which a mentally handicapped person's behaviour can impinge on the whole family and cause stress for all its members. Such stress, as we have shown, can have very serious repercussions if not handled in an understanding way at an early stage. It would have been helpful, for instance, to have been able to give emotional support for the parents early on. Besides the help that this would have provided for mother, father might have been enabled to fulfil his roles as father and husband to a more effective degree.

case 4 Peter

Peter, aged 10 years, the first (and only) child was born when his mother was aged 43 years. Her pregnancy was quite normal but she was advised by her doctor to have her baby in hospital because of her age. Peter's parents had been married for 20 years and had given up all hopes of having any children. They were therefore delighted when they learned that a baby was expected.

Peter's mother had a normal labour and delivery. When she arrived back in the ward from the labour room she sensed an aura of reservedness on the part of the nurses. Moreover, they were reluctant to let her see her son or to say why. After what seemed an eternity, a young houseman came to see her and informed her in a rather anxious manner that her baby was a Mongol child. In his agitation he added – 'I know how you must feel, but if it gets too much for you it shouldn't be too difficult to have him placed in a home'. She was extremely shocked and distressed and suggested that there must be some mistake. She then insisted on seeing the consultant – a rather off-hand person – who confirmed the diagnosis and went so far as to say that a woman of her age should expect these things to happen.

Her husband was equally distressed when he heard the news and tried to be supportive but, having heard what the Consultant had said, he began to blame himself for getting his wife pregnant.

On leaving the hospital and returning home there was a good deal of heart-searching as to what should be done. The friends with whom they talked in their desperation were divided in their views as to whether it would be best for Peter to be brought up at home or under expert care. Sensibly, one of them suggested that the whole affair seemed to have been rather badly handled in the hospital and she suggested they seek the advice of the Health Visitor when she called.

The Health Visitor, recognising the distress of Peter's parents, arranged for them to be seen at the local subnormality clinic. With the clinic's help, the situation was better understood and it was decided to keep Peter with them at home.

Despite the obvious problems which lay ahead for them all, this was a decision that they never had cause to regret. Like the majority of Mongol children, Peter was an extremely affectionate, lovable and outgoing child who captivated everybody. Nevertheless, Peter's mother always remained slightly overanxious about him, particularly when he developed rather frequent chest complaints — as many Mongol children do.

In time, Peter was able to attend a day-school for educationally subnormal children. Because he was not too severely retarded, he made reasonable and satisfying progress.

Life was made much easier for his parents because friends and relatives alike never treated Peter as other than a loving and lovable child.

We hope that the reader will have observed from this case that not only is there a great need for skilful and sensitive handling of the parents' feelings from the moment that a subnormal child is born, but that continued support from friends may work wonders. Many parents of subnormal children complain with justification that they were either not informed of the nature of their child's disability or, if they were informed, the information was conveyed in a rather cavalier manner. However, in all fairness to the medical profession, it must be pointed out that they too have feelings about such situations, but may never have been taught how to handle them. Parents who have had a subnormal child and who have experienced insensitive handling are right to complain about this, but perhaps they can learn from their own unhappy experience how difficult it is for many people to regulate their emotions in such a delicate and distressing situation.

case 5 Mr Crewe

Mr Crewe was a man in his early 40's. He had worked as a farm labourer since leaving school. All his life he had lived with his parents – his father working on the same farm. He had always been recognised as being not very bright – even a little simple – but was a steady, reliable worker who coped well under supervision.

When his father reached the age of retirement, the family had to leave the tied house in which they had lived for very many years. They managed to get a house in the local village and Mr Crewe continued to work on the farm but with looser supervision than he had previously, since he had always worked under his father's direction.

The man who replaced his father had little sympathy for Mr Crewe's somewhat slow ways of working and made it clear that he thought that Mr Crewe was just lazy, and was continually 'picking' on him. As a result of this, the other farm workers began to tease him and make him the scapegoat for everything that went wrong.

One day, one of his workmates was being particularly provocative and was teasing Mr Crewe about the fact that he never went with girls. When his mate said – 'Hasn't your old man ever told you about the birds and the bees?', this was too much for Mr Crewe to take. He picked up a pitchfork and stabbed his tormentor in the chest with it.

After this incident, he did not appear to be unduly concerned about what he had done, even at the point when he was charged with attempted murder. In the period whilst he was in custody awaiting trial, his behaviour became quite irrational and he talked a lot of 'gibberish'. His state was brought to the attention of the Prison Medical Officer who recognised Mr Crewe to be suffering from a psychotic illness (schizophrenia – see Chapter 4). After two months he recovered from the illness, but it was found on psychological testing that he was within the range of *moderate mental handicap*.

When his case came before the Crown Court, he pleaded

guilty on the advice of his Counsel. The Prison Medical Officer gave evidence as to Mr Crewe's mental condition and the Court disposed of the case by means of a hospital order. (See Chapter 10).

There are a number of interesting observations to make about this case. Firstly, the case demonstrates the fact that a mentally subnormal person can, with reasonably good sympathetic support in a non-taxing job, cope reasonably well and be a useful citizen. (It is of interest that in the not-too-distant past people as relatively handicapped as Mr Crewe tended to be 'boarded out' in farm employment. Unfortunately, this was frequently abused and they were seen as a source of cheap labour.) Secondly, the case demonstrates that for people like Mr Crewe, stressful situations should be avoided if at all possible – in this instance the stresses were the move of home and the withdrawal of his father's support. Thirdly, the reader will have observed that, as we indicated earlier in the chapter, it is possible for a person who is mentally subnormal to develop a psychiatric illness. We hope that this case-illustration may serve to underline some of the differences between mental illness and mental subnormality that were also mentioned earlier.

It is only too possible for many mentally handicapped people, by bad handling, to be 'used' to their own detriment or to be blamed for unhappiness and stress which really has more to do with the people around them. This is not to criticise the families of the mentally handicapped, because they have to deal with a great deal of stress, both physical and emotional. They also have to cope with feelings of guilt and shame, of loneliness, ostracism, aggression and helplessness. They often need help to overcome these feelings and this is not always forthcoming. In particular, the presence of a mentally handicapped child, in a family where there are other children, may cause friction and a degree of embarrassment which prevent the other children from bringing their friends into the house. Mothers in particular may well become almost housebound and they can develop feelings of hopelessness in the face of a burden that seems without end. Very occasionally, parents who feel like this murder their child and then kill themselves.

Although we applaud the move away from permanent residential care as the major solution, we are also conscious of the dangers implicit in the sometimes unthinking attempts to *make* parents keep their mentally handicapped children within the family, regardless of the damage that this may be causing to all concerned. There is no doubt that there are some cases of mental handicap that *are* better dealt with in residential settings, where the appropriate skills of caring and training are available. Until now, there has been a tendency to make 'all or nothing' decisions about care – either to keep the person at home or to have him placed in an institution. This approach is too rigid, since it is possible to provide the best care by judiciously using both resources as we indicated in the case of 'Jane.'

As emerged in relation to Mr Crewe's case, it is important that the mentally handicapped person should not be set tasks which are beyond his capabilities. This is sometimes difficult to bring about in a society such as ours, with its emphasis on credit for achievement. This is perhaps a sad comment on our current system of 'values' to which we could all usefully give some more general thought.

A final point, but an extremely important one, that we would like to make in relation to mental subnormality is the danger that parents who are prepared to look after their handicapped children may tend to 'infantilise' them and to over-protect them from risks that must be faced if they are to achieve some degree of independence. We have shown in the case of 'Jane' that consideration was given to her future, when her parents would be no longer there to care for her. It is undoubtedly true that this becomes less possible when parents over-protect their handicapped child and are afraid to let go even in small measure.

reference

Department of Health and Social Security. *Better Services for The Mentally Handicapped.* H.M.S.O. Cmnd. 4683, 1971.

recommended reading

Adams, M. and Lovejoy, H. *The Mentally Subnormal: Social Work Approaches*. Heinemann. London, 1972.

Tizard, J. and Grad, J. C. *The Mentally Handicapped and their Families: A Social Survey*. Maudsley Monograph. No. 7. Oxford University Press. London, 1961.

Tizard, J. and Tizard, B. 'The Institution as an Environment for Development' in *The Integration of a Child into a Social World*. Richards, M. P. (ed.). Cambridge University Press. London, 1972.

Heaton-Ward, W. A. *Mental Subnormality*. John Wright and Sons, 1967.

Office of Health Economics. *Mental Handicap*. London, 1973.

10 The legal aspects of psychiatric disorders

In Chapter 1 of this book we gave some indication of ways in which the law reflected changing attitudes towards the psychiatrically ill, and how fear of mentally ill people led to an undue emphasis on how to contain them, while at the same time protecting their rights. This resulted in a mass of complicated legislation which catered for the mentally ill and the mentally subnormal, as distinct entities, right up to the passing of the Mental Health Act of 1959. (In Scotland, The Mental Health (Scotland) Act, 1960.)

The Act virtually swept away all previous legislation and was designed to give the maximum encouragement to patients, suffering from any form of mental illness or disability, to seek treatment promptly and voluntarily (on an informal basis). At the same time, it attempted to ensure that there were adequate restraints and safeguards where patients, in their own interests and for the safety of others, had to be compulsorily admitted to hospital and detained during treatment. A good example of this latter point was the case of Mr Crewe in Chapter 9. It will be remembered that Mr Crewe was brought before the Crown Court on a charge of attempted murder and that the prison Medical Officer gave evidence as to his mental state. The reader will also recall that he was committed to hospital and *not* to prison. In such cases the law provides for the making of enquiries into an offender's mental state, so that he can be dealt with in the most humane manner possible.

Thus, Section 60 (1) of the Mental Health Act 1959 enables courts to make hospital orders or guardianship orders in the event of:

(a) conviction for an offence (and in certain cases without proceeding to conviction).

(b) two doctors (at least one of whom is approved by the local health authority for the purpose) stating that the offender is suffering from any of the four categories of mental disorder stated in the Mental Health Act (mental illness, psychopathic disorder, subnormality and severe subnormality) of a nature or degree *which warrants detention for medical treatment or reception into guardianship*.

(c) a hospital is willing to accept the person, or the local health authority is willing to receive the person into guardianship.

(d) the circumstances being such that an order is the most suitable method of dealing with the case.

Let us now see what happened in the case of Mr Crewe. Having established a diagnosis of 'schizophrenia in a moderately severely mentally subnormal person,' the prison Medical Officer asked one of his authorised consultant psychiatric colleagues from the local hospital to see Mr Crewe. This colleague agreed with the Prison Medical Officer's findings and also expressed agreement that, in the event of the court wishing to make a Hospital Order, he would be prepared to receive Mr Crewe into his hospital. The court accepted these recommendations and made an Order under Section 60 of the Act. Mr Crewe was taken to the hospital by a local authority social worker. The reader will have noticed that the same procedure could have been carried out in Mr Crewe's case even though he had not been mentally ill, but because of his degree of subnormality alone.

Had Mr Crewe's offence been of a less serious nature and had it been the view of the doctors that he did not require institutional (hospital) care, it would have been open to the court to make an order under the same section placing him in the *guardianship* of the local health authority. This means that in Mr Crewe's case he could have continued in his job but he would have been very closely supervised by a responsible person. It is an interesting fact that the number of guardianship orders made by the Criminal Courts each year is extremely small.

If Mr Crewe had had a previous history of violent and aggressive criminality and had the doctors considered that he was a danger to the public and there seemed to be a risk of his committing a further offence if set at liberty prematurely, the court (and only a Crown Court) could have made what is called a *Restriction Order* prohibiting his release for a specified or unspecified period of time.

It may come as some surprise to the reader to learn that the numbers of Hospital Orders made by all courts in the course of a year is very small – something in the region of 1,500. The majority of these are made in respect of persons found to be suffering from mental illness.

There are other ways in which the courts can deal with offenders who show varying degrees of psychiatric disability. It may be, for example, that on hearing all the facts of a case, and finding it proved, the court will discover that the offender is already undergoing psychiatric treatment. In such a case it may well impose a penalty (such as a fine or some form of discharge) that will enable the treatment to continue uninterrupted. The court may decide, in other cases, that a custodial sentence is necessary and ask that the prison authorities seek psychiatric treatment for the offender, though there is no obligation on the authorities to carry out such a request. Indeed, there is a regrettable lack of facilities for psychiatric treatment in many penal institutions, although there is now one special prison-hospital at Grendon Underwood in Buckinghamshire.

There is a further point to be made here. A person found

committing an offence by the police, may be found to be so psychiatrically disordered that it would be pointless to bring him before a court. For example, psychiatric hospital patients sometimes abscond and in so doing commit criminal acts. If these are of relatively minor nature it is the usual practice of the police to return them to the hospital authorities, without instituting criminal proceedings.

However, there are cases in which it is not considered appropriate, either because of the lack of severity of the offender's psychiatric disorder, or because there is no need to protect the public, to have a hospital order. In these cases the court may make it a requirement of a *probation order* that the offender receive psychiatric treatment either as an in-patient or as an out-patient. The legal requirements are contained in the Criminal Justice Act 1948 (as amended by the Criminal Justice Act 1972).[*] In brief, this form of treatment can be provided:

(1) If the patient consents (this enactment differs from the Mental Health Act in that under the latter the consent of the offender is *not* required).

(2) A hospital or other establishment will receive him and is able to provide treatment (note the similarity with the Mental Health Act provision).

(3) The oral or written evidence of *one* doctor (approved under the Mental Health Act) indicates that the offender's condition requires, and may be susceptible to, treatment but is not such as to warrant his detention in pursuance of a Hospital Order.

case 1 Mrs Dexter

Mrs Dexter, aged 60 years, was a married woman with a grown-up family, all living away from home. One day this lady was observed by a counter assistant very openly to lift a tin of soup and walk away from the counter, making no effort at concealment or to pay for the goods. She was apprehended and the police were informed, since it was the policy of this particular store to prosecute in all cases of theft.

[*] Now consolidated in the Powers of Criminal Courts Act, 1973, effective from 1/7/74.

She pleaded guilty before the Magistrate, but the Probation Officer's report indicated that this was an isolated offence and quite out of character. The report also suggested that Mrs Dexter appeared to be depressed and the Officer advised the Court that a psychiatric report might help in reaching a decision. They therefore remanded Mrs Dexter on bail, making it a requirement that she was seen at the out-patient clinic of the local psychiatric hospital. The consultant who examined her reported to the court that he considered she was suffering from a neurotic depressive illness (see Chapter 3) and that given appropriate treatment he thought she would make a complete recovery. He also stated that, in this particular case, she did not require in-patient treatment and that her offence could be reasonably explained as being due to her illness.

On receiving this evidence, the court, having obtained Mrs Dexter's consent, made a probation order for 12 months with a requirement that she underwent psychiatric treatment as an out-patient.

This case illustrates the use of the Criminal Justice Act and exemplifies the three statutory requirements already mentioned.

Notwithstanding the fairly stringent legal provisions, it is usual for the court to deal with a case in an understanding and sympathetic manner and to avoid the consequences that often flow from a criminal conviction. In such instances it might discharge the offender absolutely.

As with Hospital Orders, the courts do not make extensive use of 'Psychiatric Probation Orders.' For example, a total of some 50,000 Probation Orders are made in the course of any one year. Of these, only about 1,500 would be orders with a requirement for psychiatric treatment.

Before moving on to consider ways in which the law may be invoked to deal with mentally disordered people who have not committed offences, brief mention must be made of the other areas in which the mental state of an accused person may be taken into account, either in respect of finding him guilty or in determining sentence. We would emphasise strongly that we are not dealing with these aspects in any detail. The law concerned with the determination of responsibility for criminal acts is extremely complex and has occupied the minds and energies of lawyers, doctors and social workers for many years. In fact, at the present time, the whole question of the treatment of mentally disordered offenders is being reviewed by an expert committee under the Chairmanship of Lord Butler of Saffron Walden – a former Home Secretary.

In legal practice, there are a number of what are regarded as 'special defences' of a psychiatric nature which can be put forward in the interests of an accused person. These can be summarised as follows:

(a) *A defence of insanity:* This plea is likely to be made in murder cases and is based upon the famous and contentious *McNaughten Rules*. In brief, the court has to bear evidence and must decide:

(1) Whether the defendant performed the act or made the omission with which charged, and
(2) Whether he was insane so as not to be responsible (according to the law) for his actions.

Before the introduction into English law of the concept of 'diminished responsibility' (see below), a defence of insanity was used much more often than it is now. If a defence of 'insanity' succeeds, the most usual form of disposal is for the offender to be committed to one of the 'special' hospitals which are specially designed for the care and custody of persons having criminal and violent propensities. An order made in such cases has the same effect as a Hospital Order with restriction, made under the Mental Health Act.

(b) *Diminished responsibility:* This plea overlaps to some extent that of 'Insanity.' However, it was introduced under the Homicide Act of 1957, with a view to broadening the existing legislation. It is of interest that it can still only be used in murder cases, though there are many people who consider that it should be capable of being applied in cases of lesser severity than murder. It may be worthwhile quoting Section 2 of the Act, as this gives an indication of the way in which knowledge and understanding of mental disorders has come to be applied increasingly to the treatment of criminals.

Section 2 of the Homicide Act 1957 *states:* 'Where a person kills or is a party to the killing of another, he shall not be convicted of murder if he was suffering from such abnormality of mind (whether arising from a condition of arrested or retarded development of mind or any inherent causes or induced by disease or injury) as substantially impaired his mental responsibility for his acts or omissions in doing or being a party to the killing.'

It will be clearly seen from this quotation that there are now a wide range of factors that a court can take into account in determining responsibility in murder cases. One of the advantages of this enactment is that, if diminished responsibility is proved, a verdict of *Manslaughter* is returned. The court can then deal with the case in any way it chooses. (Readers will be aware that if a verdict of Murder is returned, the penalty is fixed by law, namely, life imprisonment.) We referred in Chapter 9 to the possibility of some parents under extreme stress killing their children. In such cases, it is not uncommon for a court to return a verdict of 'Manslaughter' and in so doing it is able to dispose of the case in the humanest possible way.

(c) *A defence of 'Unfitness to Plead':* This really means a plea of 'unfitness to be tried.' In such a case, the court has to be shown that the defendant is unable to understand the proceedings or to instruct Counsel. If this is shown to the court's satisfaction, the defendant will not stand his trial but an order will be made for his admission to hospital. Once again, this plea is used very rarely, usually in cases of murder.

(d) *The defence of 'infanticide':* This is an instance in English law where the court is given power to recognise specifically the effect of child-birth on a woman's state of mind. In recognition of the existence of puerperal psychiatric illness, it can accept the special offence of infanticide in place of murder. For such a plea to be successful, it has to be shown (a) that the mother is psychiatrically ill and (b) that she has given birth to the child in question in the past twelve months. Most cases of this kind are dealt with sympathetically, usually by means of a Probation Order.

In the brief outline we have given, the reader will see that there is a great deal of flexibility in the legal and penal systems for the disposal of mentally disordered offenders. One final point remains to be mentioned that gives further emphasis to this flexibility. Under the Mental Health Act 1959, a person already in custody, either undergoing sentence or awaiting trial, whose mental state becomes such as to require compulsory detention in a hospital may be so transferred under Sections 72 and 73 of the Act.

legal considerations in psychiatric illness not involving criminal offences

We now move on to a consideration of those other aspects of the law that can be used to safeguard the rights of the individual and to ensure that he receives treatment when his mind is in such a disturbed state that either he is unable to see the need for treatment or is unable to seek it. In illustrating the legal implications involved, we shall refer back to some of the cases presented earlier in the book and in so doing will, as it were, complete some stories that we left unfinished. We shall also present one or two new cases to illustrate legal points.

compulsory admission

For some people it is necessary to ensure that they enter hospital for treatment because 'by the very nature of mental disorder such powers must be available, as many forms of disorder destroy wholly or in part the patient's ability to understand that he is ill – a condition known as "lack of insight"' (French 1971). Many of the cases used as illustrations in this book show this lack of insight and we will now recall some of these.

In Chapter 4 the reader will remember the case of Mrs Smithers. She was the housewife who had many bizarre ideas and who became unpredictably violent. It will be recalled also that her husband became understandably frightened and sent for the general practitioner. The procedure adopted in this case was as follows: The general practitioner called in the local social worker, designated as a Mental Welfare Officer under the Act. The latter considered that treatment on a compulsory basis was required and contacted the consultant at the local mental hospital (who was approved for the purpose of instituting compulsory procedures under the Act). The consultant concurred with the view expressed by the Mental Welfare Officer and the general practitioner and decided to invoke the provisions of Section 25 of the Mental Health Act which permit a patient to be detained in hospital 'for observation for up to 28 days.' A patient such as Mrs Smithers detained under this Section could, of course, receive treatment in addition to being under observation. In her case, she agreed to stay on 'informally' after the expiration of the 28 days, but had she not done so, an application for 'treatment' in her case could have been made under Section 26 of the Act. In order for this to be effected, an application by the nearest relative is required (in this case Mr Smithers), or by the Mental Welfare Officer, who must have seen the patient within the preceding 14 days. In addition, two medical recommendations are required, given separately or jointly.

There are one or two other points to make concerning this procedure. Persons of any age may be treated under this Section. *Treatment under Order* may be authorised for a period of up to one year. The order is then renewable for three periods of one year at a time and subsequently for periods of two years at a time. The grounds for recommendation for admission under this Section are threefold and must *all* be fulfilled:

(a) The patient must be suffering from mental illness or severe subnormality or from subnormality or psychopathic disorder (but in the last two instances only if he is under the age of 21).

(b) The patient must be suffering from any of the disorders mentioned in (a) above to an extent which in the minds of the recommending doctors warrants detention in hospital for medical treatment under this Section.

(c) The patient's detention must be necessary in the interests of his own health and safety or for the protection of other persons.

...The term 'nearest relative' which we have used is defined in Section 49 of the Act in such a way that a spouse is the closest relative in the case of married people and parents in the case of single people. In other cases the nearest relative may be brother or sister, grandparent, grandchild, uncle or aunt or nephew or niece. In other words, in descending order of blood proximity.

In Section (a) above, it will be noticed that it is not possible to detain compulsorily for treatment patients suffering from psychopathy or subnormality over the age of twenty-one unless they have been ordered to be detained under compulsion by a court following an offence. (See for example the case of Mr Crewe referred to earlier.) However, if they are already in hospital under these categories before the age of twenty-one they can, if necessary, be detained on the same grounds until they are twenty-five.

In certain cases it is necessary to admit under compulsion in an emergency situation. This is possible under Section 29 of the Act whereby a patient may be detained in hospital for 72 hours. This requires an application by a relative or by a Mental Welfare Officer who must have seen the patient within the preceding three days; a medical recommendation by *one* doctor is also required. No grounds for this recommendation are laid down (as they have to be for orders under Section 26 – see above). The patient must be discharged after this period, unless he agrees to stay, or an application is made for the authorisation of a 28-day period of detention under Section 25.

Prior to the 1959 Mental Health Act, all applications for compulsory admission to hospital had to have judicial authority. This, with one exception mentioned later, is now no longer the case and magistrates are not usually involved in the admission procedures. Moreover, under the 1959 Act, even when compulsory powers are used, the documents involved in the application for admission constitute an *authorisation* for a hospital to receive the patient but do not constitute an *order* for them to do so. However, it would be rare for a hospital to refuse such admission and Regional Hospital Boards are empowered to designate certain hospitals or psychiatric units for the reception of patients in emergency situations.

Returning to the question of admission to hospital in an emergency we would refer, by way of example, to the case of Mr Wagstaffe in Chapter 4. It will be recalled that Mr Wagstaffe was a young car salesman whose behaviour became increasingly manic and ended in his smashing the showroom windows and damaging the cars. We indicated that he had been admitted to hospital under order for compulsory treatment. In fact, the powers we have described for emergency admission under Section 29 were invoked and as it was considered likely that he would refuse to stay in hospital after the 72 hours permitted, a further order was made to detain him for 28 days under Section 25 of the Act.

In addition to the procedures already mentioned, there is provision under Section 136 of the Act for a police constable to remove a person found *in a public place*, who appears to him to be suffering from mental disorder and to be in immediate need of care or control. He may remove him, if he considers it in the interests of that person or for the protection of other persons, to a *place of safety*. A place of safety is defined for this purpose as a hospital, residential accommodation provided by the local authority, a police station, or any other suitable place, the occupier of which is willing temporarily to receive the patient. There are indications that the provisions of Section 136 are used somewhat haphazardly throughout the country. In some areas, the police invoke this Section and under its provisions detain the patient for a period not exceeding 72 hours in order that he can be medically examined. In others, if there is some associated unlawful behaviour, the person may merely be arrested and brought before a court. Sometimes the police will immediately inform the Mental Welfare Officer of their apprehension of a patient and arrange for his detention under any of the Sections already outlined. Finally, a police officer finding a patient who is apparently mentally disordered and 'wandering abroad' may know that the patient has absconded from a psychiatric hospital and will merely return him to that hospital without taking any other action. It should be noted, incidentally, that a patient liable to be detained under any of the Sections we have mentioned, who absents himself from hospital without leave, may be taken into custody and returned to the hospital. However, there are exceptions to this. Thus, a psychopathic or subnormal patient over the age of 21 may not be so taken into custody after the expiration of a period of six months, beginning from the first day of his absence and, in respect of any other patient, he may not be so taken into custody after a lapse of 28 days.

case 2 Mr Brown

Mr Brown, a man in his 60's, was suffering from *paranoid schizophrenia* (see Chapter 4). He had been in and out of hospital for many years.

He was often hallucinated and although a well-known figure in his local community, his behaviour was sometimes seen as alarming in areas where he was not well-known. One day, during a phase when his hallucinations were particularly severe, he was found marching up and down the High Street, shouting at and accosting passers-by in a very belligerent manner.

A policeman was eventually called to the scene and Mr Brown was persuaded to accompany him to a local police station where he was detained and examined by the Police Surgeon and a Mental Welfare Officer. They came to the conclusion that he should be detained under order and arrangements were made for his admission to hospital under Section 25 of the Act.

So far we have described instances in which mentally disordered people have in various ways come to the attention of relatives or professional people and where it has been comparatively easy to arrange for their admission to hospital. The reader may well ask himself what happens in those cases where a person believed to be suffering from mental disorder is either being ill-treated, or neglected, is being kept otherwise than under proper control or, being unable to care for himself, is living alone. In such cases (and this is the exception to what we said earlier about the absence of judicial intervention) if it appears to a magistrate on information 'laid on oath' by a Mental Welfare Officer that a person is liable to be dealt with under the above clauses, the magistrate may issue a warrant authorising a constable to enter the premises, by force if necessary, and remove the individual with a view to making such arrangements for his treatment or care as is felt to be necessary. For example, in Chapter 5, we quoted the case of Miss Slingsby, who had become increasingly cut off from those around her and from those who were trying to help her. Had her delusional ideas not brought about her repeatedly telephoning the police in the middle of the night, but had led her instead to become reclusive and to refuse entry to all callers, it would have been possible, *as a last resort*, to invoke the provisions of Section 135 of the Mental Health Act which covers this kind of situation.

informal admission

The reader will have observed that we have outlined the procedures for compulsory admission in some detail. We must now make briefer comment on admission to psychiatric hospital on an informal basis. At the beginning of the chapter we emphasised that the whole intention of the Mental Health Act of 1959 was to give the maximum encouragement to patients suffering from psychiatric disorders to seek treatment promptly and voluntarily. Underlying the provisions of the Act is the view that mental illness should be seen as being 'just another illness', to which all of us may be liable. For this reason, the intention of the Act was to make admission to hospital easy, to avoid compulsion and the need for judicial sanctions, to avoid stigma where possible, to make treatment more readily available both in and out of hospital and to provide it expeditiously. To serve all these ends, patients are admitted on an informal basis where possible, and this implies that they enter the psychiatric hospital on the same legal footing as they enter any hospital. In fact, over 95 per cent of patients are admitted to hospital in this way. All that a sick person has to do is to indicate his willingness to accept treatment when it is offered him.

the protection of patients' rights

Once in hospital, patients' rights should be very jealously guarded and this is particularly so for patients who have been admitted under compulsion. In the latter case the procedures to be followed are rigorously laid down in the Act and they must not be departed from. For example, in the compulsory Sections already outlined, at least two people must be in agreement before a person can be compelled to enter hospital, the hospital must be willing to receive him and, perhaps more important than anything else, it has to be established that no means other than compulsory admission will meet the case.

While in hospital, patients (other than those detained by order of the court) may be discharged at any time if this is considered by the authorities to be appropriate and an informal patient can leave against medical advice if he wishes. Further safeguards are provided under the Act by recourse to *Mental Health Review Tribunals*. Membership of these tribunals consists of at least one medical, one legal and one lay member. Their duties are concerned with applications by compulsorily-detained patients (or their nearest relatives) for discharge if such discharge has been withheld by the authorities unreasonably, in the opinion of the patient or nearest relative. Although an informal patient can leave at any time, we would remind the reader that the doctor is the specialist. Careful attention should be paid to his advice for, as we saw in the case of Mr Noble (Chapter 4), to ignore medical advice can have even fatal consequences. (It will be recalled that in Mr Noble's case he was encouraged by his brother to take his discharge, left the hospital and whilst out walking on his own, threw himself under a train and was killed.)

In the case of patients detained for criminal offences, the situation is slightly different. Thus, patients detained under Section 60 of the Act are still free to leave after one year unless the doctor reports otherwise, but they also have the right of appeal to a Mental Health Review Tribunal in the face of such opposition. In the case of patients who are subject to a restriction order under Section 65 of the Act, the patient can ask the Home Secretary to take the advice of the Mental

Health Review Tribunal. The latter can *advise* discharge but cannot *direct* it.

Under normal circumstances, the affairs of patients and the management of their property are conducted by their relatives – sometimes with the help of social workers, lawyers or other counsellors. However, the Mental Health Act makes provision for a section of the Supreme Court of Judicature called the *Court of Protection* to intervene if it is shown that a person is incapable, by reason of mental disorder, of managing or administering his property and affairs. The Act requires that the Court of Protection, through its appointed officers, shall do all such things as appear necessary or expedient:

(i) for the maintenance or other benefit of the patient, or of members of the patient's family,
(ii) for making provision for other persons or purposes for whom or which the patient might be expected to provide if he were not mentally disordered,
(iii) for otherwise administering the patient's affairs.

case 3 Mr Wentworth

Mr Wentworth, a man in his middle 50's, was in partnership in a small manufacturing business. He had been admitted to a psychiatric hospital suffering from a form of pre-senile dementia (see Chapter 5) and the outlook, not surprisingly, was considered to be very unfavourable.

He was quite unable to cope with his business affairs and his wife and business partner reluctantly sought the advice of the family lawyer, who arranged for the intervention of the Court of Protection.

Medical evidence was given to the court that the patient was suffering from a progressive and irreversible mental disorder and the court took over the patient's affairs, thus enabling such financial decisions to be made as were considered best for the patient's business and partnership, as well as for his wife and dependants.

The law pertaining to these matters is extremely complex and we would advise anyone involved in a situation such as described above to seek expert help. Some of the organisations which can provide help and advice are listed in our final chapter.

reference
French, C. W. *Notes on the Mental Health Act*, 1959. (Second Edition.) Shaw and Sons. London, 1971.
recommended reading
Speller, S. R. *The Mental Health Act*, 1959. The Institute of Hospital Administrators. London, 1961.

11 General discussion and conclusions

In this book we have attempted to trace the development of attitudes towards the mentally disordered and to describe the services and legal provisions for their treatment. We were prompted to undertake its writing because we thought that the fears associated with mental illness experienced by those who came into contact with it were largely born of two factors; firstly the stigma that has surrounded it over the centuries and secondly the lack of understanding about the various types of illness as they present in everyday surroundings. We have tried to show the dangers of interpreting isolated pieces of behaviour in such a way as to prompt unfeeling and inappropriate responses, which can exacerbate the illness and militate against its resolution.

The reader will recall the fatal case of Mr Sheldon (Chapter 3) and should realise the importance of trying to understand that *changes in a person's behaviour may not simply be the result of his attitude towards those around him but may be evidence of mental ill health.* Mr Sheldon's case is rather classic in this respect, for his behaviour was interpreted by those who knew him according to *their* frame of reference rather than *his*. In many ways, the reactions that his illness produced in others could be seen as their defences against understanding it; for example, his work colleagues saw his behaviour as being deliberately intended to undermine their positions and the smooth running of the organisation, rather than as being behaviour which was largely outside his control. Thus they could 'legitimately' detach themselves from this anxiety-provoking behaviour. Mr Sheldon's case demonstrates very clearly that his colleagues' efforts to avoid anxiety, albeit at an unconscious level, in fact created more, because his 'unheard' calls for help resulted in his death.

Such a case demonstrates that had there been a better understanding of mental illness, in this case of depression, all the parties concerned might have benefited.

We have pointed out how ignorance of mental illness can tempt people into interpreting observed behaviour in a way which appears to be rational, in terms of their own life experiences. We have suggested throughout the book that, when the behaviour of a mentally disordered person is so *irrational* that the observer has no frame of reference into which he can place the behaviour, he becomes extremely perplexed and, rather than seek help for the patient, he tends to 'run away' from the situation. We have tried to show that only harm can follow from this course of action.

In a general sense, we have tried to convey to the reader the need for some knowledge, or perspective, so that appropriate action can be taken which will provide help for the sick person and for those around him.

Our mode of approach – the use of cases – has not been designed purely to help the reader to recognise illness when faced with it, but we have also deliberately included in the case-descriptions examples of the 'various helping' persons and organisations who could have become involved, such as general practitioners, social workers, personnel officers, the police, student counsellors etc. It is hoped that the reader will make use of this knowledge should the occasion ever arise. We have tried to show, too, that there is a need for anyone, who sees an individual suffering from a mental disorder, to take some appropriate action directed towards alleviating the condition. We underline the fact that the persons near to the sufferer may themselves be in need of understanding and support, so that they can be given encouragement to take appropriate action. This aspect was exemplified by the case of Peter in Chapter 9. The perplexity which surrounded the birth of this mongol child and the rather unfeeling way the information about his abnormality was handled, caused many problems, but it was demonstrated how the thoughtfulness of friends brought the advice and help of an expert. His support enabled Peter's parents to have much more hope for the future and the normal pleasures of parenthood which might otherwise have been lost.

In Chapter 10 we made the point that, even when compulsory admission is required, there is no intention to deprive people of their basic rights. This is not to say that there are never abuses of these rights (some of these were referred to in Chapter 1). There have been enquiries into such abuses and this underlines the vulnerable position in which patients so detained may find themselves and the need to remain alert on their behalf. The publicity which is attendant on these enquiries ensures that the patients' interests are being guarded, but unfortunately they sometimes produce a public feeling that *all* hospitals are badly run and that *all* patients are badly treated. It may be for these latter reasons that some relatives go against medical advice in their efforts to remove a patient from such 'dire' circumstances. We would emphasise yet again that *the abuses are the exceptions and that, in the main, hospitals are well run and are humane in their intentions.* It is for this reason that we have stressed, on several occasions, the importance of relatives being guided by the psychiatric experts.

Not only has the stigma and fear of mental disorder caused relatives and friends to act inappropriately, but these feelings sometimes prevent the maintenance of contact between the mentally sick person and his family. Given the understanding that we have tried to convey, it is hoped that the bridge between home and hospital will be maintained, not only by constantly visiting such people, but also by taking them home for short periods when this is recommended. In addition to the obvious therapeutic benefits for the patient and his family, such contact must ultimately limit the opportunities for the possible abuses we have adverted to. Recent enquiries into ill-treatment of patients have revealed that many of the individuals concerned had no personal contact with the outside world. The main intention of this book has been to try to show that mental illness should be approached in much the same way as any other illness, for, as we have demonstrated, *the majority of mentally sick people do get better with help.*

Throughout the book we have referred to a number of helping agencies. For the reader's convenience, we shall end the book by listing the better known of these whose addresses may be found in most telephone directories.

some helping agencies
(*a*) *General*
Local Authority Social Service Departments.
(Usually listed under the City or Council Authority – Area offices are also listed.)
Probation Departments.
Law Society.
Police Departments.
(Particularly where there is a Drugs Squad.)
Citizens' Advice Bureaux.
Post Offices.
(Information on welfare rights and benefits are available in leaflet form.)
Department of Employment and Productivity.
(Particularly in respect of resettlement and rehabilitation of persons suffering from mental disorder.)
(*b*) *More specific*
MIND (National Association for Mental Health.)
(There are branches throughout the country, but not in every region.)
Society for Mentally Handicapped Children.
Telephone Samaritans.
(Offers help to those persons in personal crises and particularly the suicidal.)
Alcoholics Anonymous.
Gamblers Anonymous.

Neurotics Nomine.
Regional Drug Centres.
(To be found under Hospitals.)
Local Drug Liaison Committees.
(These are not usually listed but may be contacted through the Police or local branch of the Royal College of General Practitioners.)
Cruse.
(An organisation for the help of widows and their children.)
Society of Compassionate Friends.
(Help for the dying and the bereaved.)
National Council for Civil Liberties.
(Help for persons who consider they may have been unlawfully detained.)
National Association for the Care and Resettlement of Offenders.
Howard League for Penal Reform.
These last two organisations concern themselves with offenders and their families.

recommended reading

Guide to the Social Services. Published each year by the Family Welfare Association. London.

Willmott, P. *Consumer's Guide to the British Social Services.* Penguin Books. Harmondsworth. (Latest Edition.)

Index to names and case studies

INDEX

Adams, M *174*
Aesclepiades *19*
Aichorn, A *32*
Ames, Mr 109
Arbuthnot, Mrs 66
Aretaeus *20*
Ashley, 7th Earl of Shaftesbury *25*
Aurelianus, Caelius *20*

Bakwin *27*
Banks, Mrs 55
Bass, Mr 130
Beers, Clifford *31*
Bleuler *27*
Blythe, Mr 65
Bolton, Mr 155
Boulter, Mr 62
Bowen, Mr 65
Bowlby, John *31*
Brown *23*
Brown, Mr 136
Burt, C *27*

Cameron *27*
Cartwright, Miss 147
Carver, Mr 115
Celsus *19*
Chapman, Miss 110
Charcot *26*
Clarke, A D B and A M *157*
Clarke, D S *33*
Cleckly, H *122*
Cobb, S *44*
Connolly *28*
Crewe, Mr 171
Croft, Miss 129

Department of Health and Social Security. Better Services for the Mentally Handicapped. Rept. *160*
Dexter, Mrs 178
Dix, D L *28*
Down-Langdon *167*
Dublin, L I *157*
Duncan, A *25*

Ebbing-Kraft *27*
Esquirol *25*

Family Welfare Association. Guide to the Social Services *195*
Fish, F *67*
French, C *190*
Freud, S *26*

Galen *20*
Galton *159*
George III *23*
Gillespie (See Henderson and Gillespie) *33, 67*
Glatt, M M et al. *138*
Grad, J C *174*
Grainger, Mrs 96
Grossman, I G *138*

Hall, Miss *61*
Hargreaves, Mrs *154*
Harper, Mrs 130
Harris, Mrs 93
Harvey, Mr 118
Henderson (and Gillespie) *33, 67*
Hewitt, Mr 151
Hill, Mr 72
Hippocrates *19*
Hobbs, Mr 107
Hodgson, Mr 83
Holmes, Mr 80
Holt, Mr 129
Home Office – Report on Drug Addicts *139*
Hood, Mr 114
Hunt, Mr 136
Hurley, Miss 81

Jahoda, M *44*
Janet, P *26*

Jane 167
John 165
Jones, K *33*
Jones, Mrs 47
Josephus *18*

Kahn, J H *67*
Kay, D W K *103*
Kessel, N *138, 139*
Kraepelin *27*
Kramer *21*

Langeveld, M J *44*
Lindemann, E *103*
Long, Mr 131
Lovejoy, H *174*

McCulloch, J W *86, 122, 138, 157*
Mandelkorn, P *157*
Mary 168
Maudsley, H *26*
Menninger, K *35*
Mesmer, A *26*
Meyer, A *26*
Mitchell, A *138*
Moreno *32*
Munro, A *86, 122, 138*

Nebuchadnezzer, King *18*
Noble, Mr 70
Nursten, J P *67*

Office of Health Economics
  Report on Alcoholism *139*
  Report on Drug Addiction *138*
  Report on Mental Handicap *174*

Paracelsus *22*
Paré *21*
Peter 169
Philip, A *157*
Plater, F *22*

Plato *17*
Pinel *25*

Rathod, N *138*
Rayner, E *44*
Reil *23*
Rogers, Mrs 71
Roth, M *103*
Rourke, Sgt 55
Rumbold, Mr 152
Rush *23*

***S**amson, Mr 101*
Sarbin, T R *44*
Saul, King *18*
Schneidman, E S *157*
Scott *38*
Sheldon, Mr 49
Sholto, Mrs 153
Short, Mr 135
Slingsby, Miss 99
Smithers, Mrs 82
Soranus *20*
Speller, S R *190*
Sprenger *21*
Stahl, G *23*
Stengel, E *157*
Sydenham *23*

Tizzard, B *174*
Tizzard, J *174*
Tuke *25*
Tyler, L *44*

Underwood Committee, Report of *44*

Valentine, M *44*
Vives, J *22*

***W**agstaffe, Mr 74*
Walker, Mr 112
Walton, H *139*
Ward – Heaton, W A *174*
Watson, Mrs 149

Watt, Mr 96
Webb, Mr 61
Webster, Miss 106
Wentworth, Mr 189
Weyer 22
Willcox, Mr 117
Williams, Mrs 89
Willis, Dr 23

Willmott, P *195*
Wilson, Miss 59
World Health Organisation
    Report on Alcoholism *138*
    Report on Drugs *138*
Worthington, Mr 113
Wright, Mr 54

Subject index

INDEX

Abuses – of rights of patients *25, 182 et seq.*
Addiction – see dependence *123, 133*
Adolescence *39, 41*
Adolescence – pre. *39*
Affectionless Personality *116*
Affective disorders (see depression also) *68*
Affective disorders – mood changes *69*
Aged – psychiatric disorder in *Ch. 5*
Ageing – normal processes of *87*
Agoraphobia *65*
Alcoholism, Types of *133*
Amphetamines *125*
Ancient Times, Treatment of mentally ill in *17 et seq.*
Anorexia Nervosa *58*
Anxiety – hysteria *55, 56*
Anxiety States, Main features of *53*
Anxious Personality *106*

Barbiturates *126*
Behaviour, Changes in of mentally ill patients *13*
Belle Indifference 61
Bereavement, In Elderly *91*
  Abnormal Effects of *92*
  Depression as an aspect of *93*
  Normal Effects of *91 et seq.*
  Ways of helping in cases of *94*
Board of Control *31, 32*
Brain Damage *100 et seq.*
Brain Damage, In Subnormality *164*

Cannabis *127*
Chromosomal Abnormalities – and subnormality *164*

Claustrophobia *65*
Community Psychiatry *30*
Compensation Neurosis *58, 62*
Compulsory Admission *182 et seq.*
Confusional states – in elderly *89, 90*
Cretinism *165*
Crises, Life *39*
Cyclothymic Personality *112*

Defectiveness, see Subnormality *Ch. 9*
Delusions, In Schizophrenia *79*
  In Depression *70, 76*
Dementia, Senile *87, 95 et seq.*
  Aterrio Schlerotic *96 et seq.*
Demonology *20*
Dependence, Drug *123*
  Alcohol *133*
Depression, Endogenous *46*
  Exogenous *46*
  Guilt in *47, 71*
  Mild *46 et seq.*
  Psychotic *68 et seq.*
  Reactive *46*
Depressive Personality *107*
Diminished Responsibility *180*
Dissociation *60*
Down's Syndrome *164*
Drug Dependence *123*
Drugs, Family and social background *128*
Drugs and the Law *128*
Drugs and subnormality *164*
Drugs, Profile of Takers *128*
Drugs, Trafficking In *128*

Eighteenth Century, Treatment of Mentally ill in *23*
Emergency Admission, Under M H Act 1959 *184*
Encephalitis *163*
Engagement Neurosis *58*

Epilepsy, True *102*
  Following Head Injury *101*
  Hysterical *61 et seq.*
Exhibitionism *122*

Feeblemindedness, see under Subnormality *158*
Fitness to plead – in criminal proceedings *181*
Frigidity *120*

General Paralysis of the Insane (G P I) *27, 102*
German Measles, see under rubella *163*
Guardianship, Under Mental Health Act, 1959 *176, 177*

Habituation, To Drugs *125*
Hallucinations, In Schizophrenia *79*
Handicap-Mental, see under subnormality *158*
Head Injury, Effects of *101*
Helping Agencies, *see Appendix 194 et seq.*
Heroin *127*
Homosexuality *121*
Hospital Orders – under Mental Health Act, 1959 *176 et seq.*
Hospital Period in Psychiatry *28*
Humane Reform, Period of *25*
Hypomania *73 et seq.*
Hysteria, Definition of *57*
  Main features of *57*
  and malingering *57*
Hysterical Amnesia *61*
Hysterical Conversions *61*
Hysterical Manifestations *60*
Hysterical Personality *110*

Idiocy, see under subnormality *158*
Ill-Treatment, Power to remove patient *186*
Impotence *120*
Infancy *39 et seq.*
Infanticide *181*
Informal Admission *187*
Insanity, As defence in criminal trial *180*

Learning *36 et seq.*
Lesbianism *121*
Lunacy Act, 1890 *26*
L S D *126*

McNaughten Rules *180*
Malingering, see under hysteria *57, 58*
Mania *73 et seq.*
Masturbation *120*
Meningitis *163*
Mental Deficiency Act, 1913 *29*
Mental Disorder, Fear of *14*
Mental Health Act, 1959 *31, 175 et seq.*
  (Scotland) 1960 *175*
Mental Health, Description of *34*
Mental Health Review Tribunals *188*
Mental Ill Health, Causal Factors *43*
Mental Welfare Officers *183, 185, 187*
Middle Ages, Treatment of Mentally Ill in *22*
Mongolism – See *Down's Syndrome* *164*
Monophobia *65*
Morphine *127*

Neglect, Power to remove patients in state of *186*
Neurosis, Description of *46*
Nineteenth Century, Treatment of Mentally Ill in *26*

INDEX

Non-Restraint, Period of *28*

Obsessional Personality *108*
   States *64 et seq.*
Offenders, Mentally Disordered *175 et seq.*
   Under Mental Health Act, 1959 *176*
   Under Powers of Criminal Courts Act, 1973 *178*
Opiates, see under Heroin and Morphine *127*

Paranoid Personality *114*
Paranoid Schizophrenia – see under Schizophrenia *83, 84*
Paraphrenia, Late *98*
Personality Disorders *Ch. 6 and 128*
Phenylketonuria *164*
Phobic States *46, 64 et seq.*
Place of Safety, under Mental Health Act, 1959 *185*
Primary Gain, In Hysteria *58*
Probation and Mental Treatment *178*
   Court of *189*
Protection of Patient's Rights *188*
Psychopathy *116*
Psychoses, Functional *Ch. 4*
Psychosexual Disorders, see under Sexual Disorders *119*

Radiation Hazards, and Subnormality *163*
Restriction Order, under Mental Health Act, 1959 *177*
Retardation, see under subnormality *Ch. 9*
Rubella and subnormality *163*

Sado-Masochism *121*

Schizoid Personality *113*
Schizophrenia, Description of *113*
   Main Signs and Symptoms *77 et seq.*
   Paranoid *83, 84*
School Phobia *65*
Secondary Gain, In Hysteria *58, 62*
Seventeenth Century, Treatment of Mental Illness in *22*
Sexual Disorders *119*
Subnormality, Causal factors *163 et seq.*
   Court proceedings *171, 176*
   Definitions of *160*
   Historical aspects *158 et seq.*
   And Mental Illness *158, 176*
   Recognition of *162*
   Size of problem *161*
Suicide, and Alcohol *155*
   Common misconceptions about *142 et seq.*
   Common traits of suicides *156*
   And criminality *153*
   And Depression *152*
   And emotional factors *146*
   And employment *153*
   And financial problems *151*
   And helping agencies *143, 194*
   And interpersonal relations *147 et seq.*
   And legal aspects *145*
   And social background *151*
Syphilis, see under General Paralysis of the Insane *27, 102*

Transvestism *122*

Voyeurism *121*